Seriously, Mom, you didn't know?

~

Marguerite Quantaine

C&K Publications
Published in the United States
3050 NE 55th Ave, Silver Springs, FL 34489-0925

ISBN 13: 978-0-940548-05-3

First Edition

Cover art adapted by M.J. Cantine from an unsigned 1913 French postcard.

Seriously, Mom, you didn't know? contains refreshed passages originally published and previously copyrighted by Marguerite Quantaine © 1976-2018 in *The Arts & Antiques Antiquarian, Imogene's Eloise: Inspired by a true story, The St. Petersburg Times, The New York Times, More ezine, and Venus ezine © 2011* and @ www.margueritequantaine.com.

CONTENTS

~ In Loving Memory ~
Baby Kate

PREFACE

My patriarch surname was changed from the original French spelling to English when my ancestors emigrated here during the late 1600s. While mine was an uncommon name in modified English until the turn of the 21st century, it was also so easy to pronounce that I spent the first half of my life baffled by the majority of those who *mispronounced* it, even after being corrected. It was as if they weren't taught the basic English 101 rule of 'e' on the end makes the 'i' say 'i.' In exasperation I reverted to the original French spelling, adding an 'e' to the end as a qualifier. Now, no one bothers trying to pronounce my last name correctly, automatically opting for a more matriarchal manner of addressing me as simply, Marguerite. I am my mother's namesake. It suits me best.

THE LOOK OF LOVE

I'm a ninth-generation American homosexual.

Either that or there's an amazing number of spinsters and bachelors in my ancestry. I count the potential for several in every generation on both sides of the family over the past 350 years.

Perhaps that's why the stigma attached to being single wasn't an issue in my upbringing. My father's sister never married. And even though the topic of why wasn't openly broached, my maternal grandmother divorced after her second daughter was born. She spent the balance of her life as single, in the close company of women.

I suppose you could misconstrue this as proof that it's possible to be raised gay, or that I was. But you'd be wrong. I wasn't raised to be sexual at all. Like so many of my generation, the subject of sex was taboo in our home. And even though I grew up with two sisters and three brothers, we never shared conversations of an intimate nature until we were all well into our forties. Even then, the conversations between us were strictly casual.

My father was as distant by choice as my mother was demonstrative by nature. It was she who showed us how happiness flows from doing good. We learned to be courteous, courageous, curious and kind. We were exposed to music, literature, art and theater. We were trained to respect language through oratory and debate. And while exploring the works of William Shakespeare, my mother implored us to hold dear the line, "To thine own self be true."

So don't think it took some long struggle with my sexual identity before I spoke the words "I'm gay" to my mom. Nor was it her fear of hurting my feelings that kept an exchange from happening before she reached 89.

It's simply — believe it or not — most lesbians I've encountered don't consciously categorize themselves as being such, per se. I know I don't. I never have.

True, I avoided dating while in high school and remained chaste until halfway through my 23rd year. By then the family phone fêtes had my younger sister convinced I was a recluse while my older sister swore I must be *on* something (or should be).

Hence, when I called home from New York City that glorious March day in 1970 to tell Mom I'd be bringing a friend back for a visit, she was delighted. She didn't question what the relationship entailed or which gender it involved. All that mattered was I'd finally connected with someone.

No one has questioned it since. Elizabeth remains the only love of my life. For the past 49 years, we've lived under the same roof sharing the same bank account, abiding by the same ethics, collaborating in the same businesses, supporting the same candidates, and demonstrating the same respect and affections for an array of animals.

We've never been purposely apart in all those years. Never taken separate vacations, or wanted to. Never appeared at gatherings alone. Never accepted an invitation unless the other's name was included on the envelope. Never sent a birthday card, letter, or holiday greeting without our joint salutation.

We aren't provocative or particularly political. There's no role-playing, recognition-dressing, or exhibitionism. And, even though our choice to remain reserved is based on a noth-ing-to-hide-nothing-to-share ideology, you can't exactly clas-sify us as closeted.

The fact is, a rare few have ever asked us, "Are you gay?" Instead, we've been treated like any other two people who graciously appear as an extension of the other.

But then, at age 89, Mom finally brought it up.

"Why now?" I asked her during our daily long-distance chat.

"I watched a biography on television last night about two men who had this great devotion for each other," she recounted. "And I marveled at how wonderful it must be to know that kind of love. It made me think of you and Liz."

My eyes welled.

"But they led such tragic lives in many ways," she contin-ued. "I hope no one's ever been mean to you like that."

I recognized a question masked in those words.

. . .

Mom and I were always close. She was a role model for the independent spirit I became, a mentor of uncommon good sense, and a show of courage in the face of futility. But there are things I'd never confided — mostly because they all occurred to me in retrospect, long after I'd missed the meaning of the stone thrown.

I recall I'd just turned 15, fresh from being voted the wittiest girl in my class and slated to become editor of the school paper, a forensics champion, pantomimist, and finally, most photographed face in my senior yearbook. Plus, some considered me cute to boot.

Yet I was never a team player. I rarely attended school events. I avoided pep rallies. I didn't spend after-hours with classmates. I resisted temptation and defied intimidation, refusing to follow the crowd. And I simply *didn't* date.

It's not that I lacked opportunity. Indeed, my primary pals were male. But I was careful to keep boys at bay, preferring platonic relationships restricted to school hours or clustered occasions. Because my mind wasn't functioning in the immediate present back then. It was clouded with illusions of running off to New York's West Village to live as a Bohemian poetess and consumer underachiever.

One afternoon while stopping to pick up books for history class, I noticed a word scrawled sideways down my hallway locker, with letters the six-foot length and one-foot width of the door: Q-U-E-E-R.

It was 1961, at a time when queer wasn't generically derogatory in small-town, Midwest America, and graffiti was mostly an anomaly. I pondered the purpose of the scribbling for only a moment before shrugging, grabbing my books, and jamming the combination lock closed.

Then I glanced toward the far end of the hall where my best friend stood in the company of girls belonging to the most popular class clique. They seemed insidious standing there, watching me. Watching as I approached my locker. Watching as I read the message on the door. Watching while I prepared to leave.

So I did the unexpected. I waved, smiled, and walked away — oblivious.

Because right then, I hadn't a clue the day would dawn when I'd look across a crowded room and fall in love with the woman looking back at me.

Although, apparently, *they* knew — those cowards with 'pencils' mightier than swords.

"No," I said to calm my disquieted mother. "No one ever hurt me."

It was such a long time ago and such a well-intended little lie.

But I think about it more often now that she's passed on and I'm getting older. How the heartsore hasn't healed much in the centuries since the first of my ancestors sought freedom here from religious persecution. How women are still raped and ridiculed, and men are still mauled and murdered in righteous retribution for being gay.

What has changed is an emergence of people demonstrating enlightenment, compassion, acceptance, and moral courage — albeit most of them parents, friends, and relatives persuaded by science and genetic codes.

Oh sure, I know there will always be conflict between

those who flash a swagger as their badge of honor and those who flash a swish. But I'm thinking, someday, there might be three key identities from which to choose: Heterosexuals. Homosexuals. And people who love each other.

The last one?

That would be me.

\# \# \#

This refreshed essay copyrighted by Marguerite Quantaine © 2002 first appeared in The St.Petersburg Times.

## 2

THE FINE ART OF NAME-CALLING

*M*y college roommate, Gloria Tata, called me Magpie. I didn't understand why at the time, having only associated the word with that of a large, black, squawking bird.

At 5'1" and 90 pounds, fair skinned and auburn-haired, I didn't see myself as a crow any more than I saw her as a Po-Ta-Ta, a nickname that sprang to mind, but was never uttered because I instantly censored it as knee-jerk, uninspired, and possibly used to taunt during her schoolyard years.

Instead, I simply changed the inflection and called her Ta-Ta, as if saying 'so long' or 'goodbye' whenever greeting her.

I first met Gloria one afternoon at the Wayne State University Student Union in Detroit after buying the last piece of cherry pie, my least favorite, just before a cafeteria worker put out plates of blueberry, my pie of choice. The place was so packed it took a while to find a seat, and when two were finally vacated, Gloria plopped down beside me, each of us spying a preferred pastry on the others tray.

"Trade?" we said, simultaneously. It initiated both our friendship and a series of subsequent exchanges, beginning with each other's winter coats that we traded on the way out of the Student Union.

At the end of the semester, I was ordered to find other lodgings as the penalty for missing my ten o'clock curfew at the dormitory one night and awakening the dorm mother by howling like a desolate dog. It was just as well. I felt suffocated living on a hallway of freshwomen who joined ranks to form instant cliques concentrated on rushing various sororities.

Fortunately, a two-room plus cubbyhole and bath unit opened up on the third floor of the only independent apartment building left standing on campus that I happened by at the exact moment the superintendent placed a 'For Rent' sign in the lobby window. Knowing I couldn't afford the place alone, I signed on the dotted line, certain of Gloria's willingness to join me. She did.

Gloria looked remarkably like Marisa Tomei (who wasn't born until December of that year so, technically, Tomei would come to look remarkably like Gloria). She was a good-looking, straightforward, high-spirited girl whose only college aspiration seemed to be that of finding a man — which she did within a matter of months. Never mind that he appeared to me as an older, somewhat slovenly, heavyset biker. To Gloria, her Chantilly perfume and peppermint gum-smacking complemented his black leather jacket and motorcycle boots.

I don't know what became of Gloria. She left without warning atop biker-boy's back seat, her long black hair tied with a red bandana and all her belongings stuffed into a brown paper bag. But the memory of her and that term of endearment still lingers, even though I never met another Tata and no one ever called me Magpie again.

Instead, people refer to me with a variety of other monikers. My siblings call me Madge, Marge, Margie, Jill (my middle name), and Willish (for my willingness to accept dares from my brother Kit.) My grandma called me Little Marguerite. A high school friend nicknamed me The Little Red Fox. Different people have addressed me as both Marjorie and Morningstar (though never together), Megan, Smadge, Missy, McQ, Midgie, Ginger, Red, and Blush. Two longtime, older female friends in their eighties still refer to me as The Kid, and an illustrator chum from way back called me Opal.

But my sweetheart mostly calls me Pumpkin, and there wasn't a day gone by in her lifetime that Mom didn't call me Dolly.

Regardless, I'm thinking maybe Gloria was the one who got it right from the get-go.

magpie : noun 1. a long-tailed crow with boldly marked plumage and a raucous voice. (It fits, albeit my plumage is auburn. As for my loud voice, it tends to crow about almost everything.)

2. used in similes to refer to a person who chatters idly. (So I'm told and may have proven it here.)

3. Origin, late 16th century: Middle English nickname for the given name of Marguerite + pie.

Fair enough.

I'll have whatever you're having.

# # #

A RARE AND VALUABLE COMMODITY

hile watching a rerun of *The Antiques Roadshow* broadcasting from Tulsa, I got a message from my friend, Frances Walker Phipps. It was sent to me from infinity and beyond, but arrived just fine. No dropped call.

Frances was a reporter for several Connecticut newspapers, the antiques columnist for *The New York Times Connecticut Weekly*, the author of several definitive reference books on American antiques and colonial kitchens, and the founder of *The Connecticut Antiques Show* (1973) and touted as one of the five most prestigious such events in the nation. Renown as a barracuda among a tribe of elite dealers who vied for the chance to earn a space in her much-envied function, Frances determined what could or could not be displayed on the show floor; what was or was not an authentic antique. Her strict vetting of booth merchandise on preview night was surreptitiously referred to as the Phipps "reign of error."

The Tulsa Roadshow featured a woman who presented a folk art doll for discovery.

I don't own a folk art doll, but I do have a folk art cat that Frances gave me from her private collection of antiques dating from the 17th and 18th century, like most of the chairs, tables, cupboards, beds, books, and decorations in her Haddam, Connecticut, home. Hand stitched from swatches of forget-me-not floral broadcloth and twisted black yarn to form it's Queen Anne stylized eyes, nose, mouth, whiskers, and outline of front legs with four toes, the coveted cat is in remarkable condition, even with the two small tears near its right eye, and drops of dried blood near its heart. I suspect the cat is older and rarer than the rag doll the *Roadshow* appraised at fifteen hundred dollars.

Their assessment made me smile. Not for the price it garnered, but for what Frances said in my head: "Bull."

Frances Phipps was once an attractive woman with thick, wavy hair, a bright smile, a great mind, and a fervor for the preservation of Colonial Americana who, by the time we first met, had matured into an unpretentious, stout woman with a big bust, a fierce wit, an untamed tongue, attired in rumpled clothes, a bad wig (pulled down like a wool cap onto her head), and a folded over Kleenex stuffed behind the right lens of her black horn-rimmed glasses to hide a socket ravaged by a malignant tumor.

We were introduced by her ex, Midgie Donaldson, on the opening night of *The Connecticut Antiques Show* in 1975 when I was the editor of a fledgling magazine, *The Arts & Antiques*

Antiquarian, and she was the highly respected authority, wielding power and influence over dealers selling to the rich and famous.

"So you came here thinking I'd teach you all about antiques. Is that it?" she proposed.

"No-o," I smart-alecked. "But I heard you have an eye for it."

It bonded us, instantaneously.

Back then, those of us in love with another woman conducted our lives without a need for labels or social acceptance. One simply knew by the level of trust demonstrated and access allowed who was or wasn't in 'the life.' That knowledge was enough to make you either relax your behavior to match the respect given, or strengthen your guard wherever zealots loomed. The antiques trade has always had its share of both, but nothing interferes with doing business.

One summer morning, a year later, my Elizabeth accepted a luncheon invitation to Francis' beach house in Westport, about ninety minutes from our Huntington, New York, home. After we'd driven the 29 miles of the Long Island Expressway, crossed over the Throgs Neck Bridge, exited onto I-95, and traveled another 30 miles toward Stamford, I glanced at the telephone number we were given to call once we got in town.

"This isn't a Connecticut number," I noted while pulling an Esso map out of the glove box to search the index.

"Meaning what?"

"This area code is for Westport, *Massachusetts.*"

"So?"

"*So?* It's another 150 miles down the road, that's what's so!"

"Oh, like I was supposed to know that?"

"You might have asked."

"I didn't want to look stupid."

"Oh, sure. I get it. As if accepting a lunch date in the morning from someone 250 miles from Huntington registered as smart. Uh-huh."

It was after four when we finally dragged ourselves through the door of the beach house. But before I could offer an explanation or apology, Frances hurled a cotton stuffed calico cat at me and smirked, "That's for making the crack about my eye for antiques!"

"Oh yeah?" I sputtered, instantly understanding the game. "Well then I'm keeping this ratty old rag cat!"

"As intended, my dear. As intended."

In April of 1986, on the morning of *The Connecticut Spring Antiques Show* evening opening, we didn't find Frances in her MANAGER ONLY curtained cubbyhole at the back of the Hartford Armory auditorium.

"She might still be at the hospital," suggested Midgie. "She's not due here until noon."

A feeling of foreboding overcame us, so we drove down to the hospital and requested her room number.

"You can't see her right now," a nurse told us, visibly shaken. "She was accidentally given a double dose of chemo. The doctors are with her now."

"Will you tell her we're here?'

"Whom shall I say…"

"Marge and Liz. Tell her we're right here waiting for her."

Hours later, after the three p.m. shift change, a different nurse asked, "Are you here to see someone?"

"Frances Phipps."

"Are you family?"

"No. Friends."

"I'm sorry, but only family members are allowed to see or inquire about Miss Phipps. Hospital rules."

By the time we left Hartford that night, there was still no word of Frances. The gala had gone off without a hitch.

It was well past midnight when we finally got home and nearly noon before we heard the news that Frances had passed away. Her obituary said she died of a heart attack at 62.

Bull.

Here's the thing: Our existence evolves through exchanges, most of it involving how we choose to spend our time in pursuit of people, places, or things on which we place the greatest value. Just as the woman at *The Antiques Roadshow* planned to sell her ancestor's rag doll to ensure her present, so did Frances Phipps plan on preserving her 200-year-old calico cat to ensure her memory. Ultimately, life is calculated — not by what we let go of from our wallets, but by what we hang onto with our hearts.

Rag doll: $1,500

Rag cat: Priceless

# # #

## 4

SECRETS & TIES

*M*arion Deyo didn't exactly start out as my friend or finish up as such. And yet, now, decades after our final exchange, the ending to our story remains astounding.

We met in 1966 when I was a student at the American Academy of Dramatic Arts, desperately searching for a different dream. It's not that I didn't enjoy acting. I did. In fact, my audition instructor, the late great Jessica Tandy, said I had the natural talent to guarantee a bright future in the theater.

But I knew I didn't have the personality for it — particularly the New York City five-floor walk-up, noisy neighbors, bug-infested-living part. Or the 'menial labor between parts' part. Or the 'suck up and shut up' part, the 'waiting for hours to audition with those who actually wanted to wait for hours to audition' part, the 'desire for fame and fortune' part, the 'tediousness of tapping feet and twiddling thumbs while slow learners remembered their lines' part, the 'talk among actors about nothing but acting' part, and the 'throw Momma under the bus to get the part' part.

It's why I applaud (but never became a fan of) celebrities. I know how hard they work to arrive at wherever they end up. I know of the bad choices they generally make. I know some struggle to get by in the public eye. I know how self-destructive many become when disdaining fellow actors.

But I digress.

One Stouffer's morning dominated by a hot buttered pecan roll and golden cup of coffee in hand, an ad for a media clerk at a Fifth Avenue agency in *The New York Times* classifieds caught my eye. I didn't know what the job entailed but reasoned clerks keep records. Enough said.

Upon entering the office of the department head assigned to interview me, I zeroed in on her desktop nameplate: Marion Deyo.

The older woman (by 21 years) didn't look up. She didn't ask me to be seated. She didn't make any attempt to put me at ease. She even forced me to introduce myself to the top of her bent down head, busily engaged in reading my job application.

"I've never heard of anyone with your last name," she muttered.

"Oh yeah?" I volleyed back. "Well, I've never heard of anyone with *your* last name, either!" It was an instantaneous, pompous reaction that I don't know why I had since — then as now — I've yet to encounter a single person outside my immediate family who has my last name.

Suffice it to say, the interview ended abruptly, and I went on my Mary-quite-contrary way until a week later when I got an early bird phone call.

"You're hired," the voice declared.

"How?" I asked. "And why?"

"No one else applied for the job," replied the person who would spend a fast five minutes training me that same day.

Technically, Marion was my boss, but she never spoke to me, making a point of ignoring me whenever we were in the same room or passed in the hall.

Cue Ruth Ruffino (a fictitious name in this otherwise true story). Ruth was a four-foot-eight gentile yenta with coal black hair to match her widow-wear-daily outfits. She had a Pattypan squash complexion, half-dollar size eyes, and a passive-aggressive control freak personality that she conveyed through a chronically clogged nose. Ruth was transparently disingenuous, cloying, suffocating, and every bit the type of women I disdain.

Nevertheless, Ruth was a popular Miss nicey-nicey, chirpy-chirpy, brown-nosey to others, buying the favor of our communal office of eight women by supplying them with free donuts most mornings and coffee every afternoon.

Women engaged shoulder-to-shoulder in one room always have their eyes peeled and ears cocked. It provides the ideal stage with an instant audience for someone working the crowd, which Ruth always did. Whenever I left the office, she made the uninvited habit of leaving a box of candy, personal note, or annoying tchotchke on my desk — yelling from her desk, "Did you get the gift I left?" when I returned.

Oh-h, I got it all right. I just didn't give it. I didn't eat the donuts, drink the coffee, accept the gifts, read the notes, or engage in conversation, even when she was hovering over me, talking at the top of her elastic sacs.

Undeterred, flowers were delivered to my apartment — not by a florist — but by Ruth herself. She left the bouquet and card with my landlord.

The next day, she crowed, "I was late to work yesterday morning because I rode all the way uptown to deliver you flowers. Did you get them?"

"Yes," I cawed back, "and assured the landlord the flowers were for him. I gave him your telephone number, just as you requested."

Soon after, Marion summoned me into her office to tell me she was letting me go for causing too many problems in her department.

To my chagrin and our surprise, I burst into tears, blubbering my side of the story from the minute Ruth laid eyes on me until my moment of breakdown there before her.

Marion listened, stone-faced, until I finished. Then she offered me a tissue and said she'd handle it — which she did. But she never said how, we didn't speak of it again, and I wasn't fired.

Hours later, Ruth announced her sudden engagement to a tall, dweeby, much older account executive who wore his suspenders and pants up around his atrophied pecs; a bloke who'd been transferred to our Chicago office that very same day, taking Ruth to the windy city with him.

The communal room of women shunned me afterward.

Over the next six weeks, I was assigned a task no other employee had been able to complete. I tackled it by initiating an unorthodox protocol, earning me a promotion and my own office.

Upon becoming Marion's executive colleague, the walls came tumbling down. We sat together at department head meetings and lunched together regularly. She learned I was single and living in Manhattan. I learned she was single and living with her cousin on Long Island. The weekend she invited me out for a visit began a quintessential friendship lasting for years — right up until the day I discovered the two women weren't cousins, but a couple.

I'd had an inkling about Marion but could never understand why everything suddenly changed between us after that. She found excuses to end our daily routine. I ceased being invited to her home. Marion took another job at a different agency. Eventually, so would I.

Over time, we continued to touch base, but seldom, until not at all.

I fell in love, and my life took many dramatic turns. We ended up living on Long Island in the same town as Marion and her partner. The company we launched and grew was in stark contrast to the enterprise they undertook. For fifteen years, we rarely crossed paths. In 1990, we semiretired to Florida. They remained on Long Island.

Then, in October of 1994, I had a premonition. It prompted me to write Marion a long letter saying how much I loved the two of them and always would. Essentially, I thanked

Marion for being my friend and confidante during a still-single period of my life when I needed guidance and protection the most. I mailed the letter. I don't know for certain if she ever received it.

But a week or so afterward, I began getting phone calls at odd hours of the day, once or twice weekly, from someone who just listened to my voice and stayed on the line for as long as a minute before hanging up. I sensed it was Marion. It *felt* like her. Week after week, call after call, for five months.

In late February of 1995, the phone calls mysteriously ceased. But it wasn't until what would have been Marion's 70th birthday in May that her partner called to say Marion had passed away on February 28th.

I immediately got online and searched for Marion's obituary. There wasn't one — so I dug deeper.

This is all I ever found:

During the late 1600s, the first woman fleeing France to America with Marion's surname married the first man fleeing France to America with my surname. We shared their DNA and subsequent ancestry.

Marion Deyo was my cousin.

# # #

## 5

IF YOU'VE EVER LOVED A DOG

*E*very year at this time, I use a luminescent-ink marker to highlight the kitchen calendar in memory of a miniature, copper-tinged Pekingese that was thrust into the arms of my partner one gusting, sleety night by a battered woman we barely knew. Hastening backward, she shrieked that her husband had beaten her and now he vowed to kill her dog.

Liz buttoned the trembling puppy inside her coat to ward off quitclaim and cold, later presenting him to me as having "followed" her home.

"Uh-huh. He just tagged along after you," I supposed before learning the dire details.

"How utterly desperate that woman was," Liz sighed.

"Dear little earth-angel," I whispered and kissed as tears filled my eyes. "From now on, you'll be our Tagalong."

We shared a fast affinity, Tag and I. Liz could feed, bathe and walk him, but most of his time was spent moored to me.

Besides being irresistibly small, courageous, and cute, three particulars made Tag precious. First, he'd been born on Liz's birthday, ensuring endearment. Second, he adored me. (Enough said.) Third, he could talk.

Yes. *Talk*. And I could understand him. Perfectly.

Whatever he said came into my head, and whatever entered my head, came out of my mouth as what he wanted known, done, or felt. A kind of oratory by osmosis.

The talk was just between the two of us at first, but eventually, we let Liz in on it. Then my mom. Then my sisters, and so forth. As word spread, we gained a following, albeit essentially esoteric. Family, friends, and neighbors were ever eager to hear Tag talk. Most were mesmerized. A few were dubious. But only skeptics dismissed us as a slick trick.

Initially, even Liz vacillated, since I never struggled to decipher the dog's din. The warble of his words would emerge clear from my mouth, almost simultaneously. Then one wee hour of a mid-March morning as the wind whipped at the windows, lightning struck power lines, and thunder menaced, Tag began to whine, chant, and drone with mouth waggling, head bobbing, and paws pawing.

"What's happening?" Liz growled, preferring the coziness of covers to dealing with predawn disasters.

"He says the upstairs porch is leaking. Rain's coming in through the sunroom ceiling."

"Dogwash," she spat, adamant.

But Tag persisted.

So Liz donned a robe and snarled her way down the stairs, words burning blue behind her. Defiantly, she flung open the

French doors to the sunroom where — sure enough — water showered the floor.

Now!" she conceded as we positioned buckets and mopped up the mess, "I'm a believer."

Tag's primary requests centered on the mundane: meal preferences, walking routes, water refills. He'd warn us of impending storms, and unexpected visitors, strays needing assistance, and strangers in the neighborhood. But his forte was in caring for me.

Years earlier, I'd been hit by a drunken driver. It left me with chronic disabilities, the worst being a brain blow that oddly augmented my faculties. These new, acute sensitivities to smell, sound, taste, and touch often-triggered agonizing seizures.

Tag could foretell an attack. In hastening me to lie down, he'd cover my forehead with his chin, creating a tranquility that somehow tempered the intensity of the spasm's fury. As if a godsend.

In the spring of 1990, Tag turned thirteen. That can be particularly old for a miniature Peke. He endured heart problems, arthritic flare-ups, and had gradually lost his eyesight and hearing. Still, Tag assured us the meds our vet prescribed kept him comfortable.

I began chauffeuring him around the neighborhood in my bike-basket so he could whisker the breeze and savor the fragrances of friends. He'd have me stop to study clouds, observe birds, or chat with cats and passersby, always intuiting those who harbored treats. We'd become a color-coordinated spectacle to behold by then, with matching bandanas and a cache of news to share. Neighbors were known and greeted by the names of their pets, earning Tag wags and purrs along the way.

One late October afternoon, as we lounged on reclining deck chairs beneath the backyard oaks, Tag inched up from where he reigned on my lap to tender my attention by gently placing his paw on my lips before softly caroling.

Liz asked, "What?"

"He says he loves us. But he has to go now. He says, don't fret. He'll be back. Tomorrow."

The tiny, pale pink tip of his tongue tasted my face one final time before he died. And in that instant, I damn-near did, too.

Make no mistake. My love for animals is immeasurable. They're my dear friends, with each loss scarring a part of my heart.

But losing Tagalong utterly crushed it.

The next night, as I crouched in a corner of our upstairs sleeping porch, still sobbing and swearing that I'd never go through such soul-wrenching sorrow again, the screech of brakes and the sound of doors slamming brought me to my feet in time to see two miscreants drag an old and crippled Irish setter from the trunk of their car and dump it in our drainage ditch before speeding off.

Instinctively, I rushed to the dog — so ruthlessly betrayed. We named him Blue. He'd be our comrade for three more years when aiding abandoned animals became our sacred-something-to-do forevermore.

All this was ruminating in my mind when I got a sweet feeling just before the phone rang one morning.

"You might not remember me," the voice quavered, "but I was the woman whose Pekingese you rescued once." A crony from our distant past had traced us and coaxed her to call.

"Did anyone ever rescue you?" I'd wondered it for thirty years.

"It took that dog to get me to go," she confessed, wounded. Still. "But I never looked back. Except for feeling grateful to you."

It begged the question: "How did you know he'd be safe with us?"

"You'll probably think I'm crazy, but…" She hesitated. "He told me."

# # #

This refreshed essay by Marguerite Quantaine © 2006 first appeared in The St. Petersburg Times.

## 6

THE THIRD TIME I DIED

I generally avoid talking about dying, having coped with living on borrowed time for most of my life. I don't discuss the actual deathblows, nor whatever followed them.

True, I did write the last experience down soon after it occurred; copious information, complete with diagrams and a glossary of terms totally foreign to me. And, yes, the person I shared it with listened, probably with skepticism — especially since my story happened twenty years before any disclosures of near-death tales became common ground.

The thing is, mine wasn't a *near*-death. Mine was a death-death experience that doesn't exactly duplicate what others have echoed to the awe and applause of audiences everywhere.

So, let me go back far enough for long enough to tell you *just* enough and nothing more.

· · ·

The first time I died was of pneumonia in 1946, two months after I was born, when the incidence was still the leading cause of infant mortality in America. According to my grandmother, I was rushed to the hospital, revived, attended to, and discharged after doctors declared there was nothing more that could be done.

While some would contend it was my grandmother's endless attention that eventually saved me, she insisted otherwise.

"It was a yellow onion," she assured with a Swedish intonation, her hair braided and pinned to her head like a peasants crown from the country she refused to speak of and claimed not to know. "On your chest."

I never understood the significance of that pungent bulb's role until recently when I read that an onion begins to absorb all viruses and bacteria in a room the moment it's cut. Nonsense? Perhaps. Nevertheless, I've been known to place a raw onion on the nightstand next to my bed at the first inkling of a cold in hopes of sleeping more soundly and awakening well — or at very least breathing better.

The second time I died, I was six weeks shy of my fifth birthday. While playing with our dog, an Irish setter named Clancy, I chased a red ball out into the street where I was struck by an oncoming taxicab. I vividly recall gleefully running, Clancy, the ball, the sandstone ledge I scooted off, the cement sidewalk with its chalk drawn hopscotch squares, the sunbeams filtering through the still leaves of a chestnut tree, my exuberance on that August afternoon, the dense, prismatic glass of headlights, a shiny chrome grill, and feeling mystified just before being hit.

I don't recall dying or anything happening directly afterward.

But I can still see — just as clear as can be — me standing near the porcelain sink in the kitchen of our century-old home, becoming oddly aware of myself with my mom behind me as she gently ran a wide-tooth comb through my hair and tying it with ribbons. My hair was long. The comb was pink. The ribbons were yellow.

"May I have a glass of water?" I whispered.

"Did you say something, Dolly?" she answered in disbelief.

"Water."

I wasn't rushed to a hospital after being hit. Instead, I was snatched up from where I'd landed several feet further down the street, carried into the house, and laid out. I don't know how long I remained motionless while Clancy stood guard or who came and went. I don't even recall regaining the perception of consciousness. All I was told is that phone calls were made, blame was assigned and reassigned, and those who were present writhed and waited until I eventually arose and walked to the kitchen, deaf, dumb and blind to it all. It might have taken minutes, or hours, or days — who knows? Because once the ordeal ended, the incidence was closed for discussion, except as a matter-of-fact briefing whenever a neighbor inquired as to my well-being.

It wasn't until twenty-one years later and the third time I'd died that I knew I might not have truly died the first two times. Yes, I'd been clinically dead by medical standards. But what doctors didn't know then and don't know still is — it was only upon dying the third time that I actually departed. The third time wasn't a *near*-death. I was totally gone. What happened to me while gone changed my life forevermore. When I reappeared after the third time dead, I knew where I'd been and instantly understood the burden a blessing of immortal insight bestows.

Seven Post-its: (1) Immortal insight *is not* something you reveal to anyone unless you're in the presence of a person or animal near death that expresses fear by words, gestures, or conduct. (2) Details pertaining to the experience *are not* something you brag about, or (3) go on talk shows staking claim to, or (4) appear in houses of worship professing. (5) Immortal insight *is not* to be exchanged for financial gain, or (6) to obtain any degree of power, or (7) used as a means to ennoble oneself.

But this I can attest to without reservation: We were given the gift of life and the unbounded ability to do our best, with endless opportunities to embrace and appreciate the here-and-now over any promise of tomorrow.

Okay, that's all. I'm done, finished and through.

Except to say, the third time I died, I sat in a VW Bug that got broadsided by three tons of 70mph speeding steel — a taxicab with an iron reinforced front bumper. My airtight car burst before sailing ten feet into the side of a building.

That might account for something.

# # #

## 7

LIE TO ME

*K*ids aren't stupid. They know we're being deceptive about bullying. They see how pervasive it is. They feel offended by the pretense of otherwise, and abandoned by the denial it exists — especially those children who endure the ridicule of a parent using words as weapons.

I know I did.

Fortunately, my mom taught me to prevail by helping me deflect criticism with the equanimity of courage and levity that best prepared me for the external world. Yet, like most kids, I felt a need to protect my mom. That's why she never knew my kindergarten teacher was a bully.

I'd been enrolled at Helmer elementary school, an 1890-built brown brick building in the public education system that flew a coveted green Safety Flag above the Stars and Stripes, raised together each morning to wave as symbols of pride over the grass and tar-top playground. The Safety Flag sported a white silhouette of a stick-figure child. It represented the student body holding the record for the longest accident-free period in the district. Helmer flew the flag for at least twenty consecutive years before I began kindergarten in 1951. But since I'd been hit by a car while chasing an irresistible red ball five weeks earlier, the flag was taken down and given to their cross-town rival, Cascades Elementary.

As requital for my misfortune, I was shamed daily by my kindergarten teacher, Miss Beech, who announced my folly on the first day of class, separating me from the circles of instruction, insisting I move my rest period rug to a solitary area, making me take my milk and cookies break alone, and relegating me to a chair in the corner during art activities — thereby branding me as unwanted and unnecessary.

"I wish you'd died," was the daily whisper to me by one classmate during recess. Eventually, she stopped and probably forgot. But I never have.

Except for my time at Helmer, I remember all my grade school teachers fondly.

By the second semester of second grade, our family moved across town to the Cascades school district where I was instantly welcomed as the student responsible for their claim to Safety Flag fame. That memory still makes me smile. But by then, I'd already learned, self-confidence and resiliency was the best defense against bullies.

So when my Girl Scout troop leader fostered intimidation by flagrantly favoring girls whose parents were members of the Country Club, I resigned and penciled a letter of complaint to the council. It wasn't acknowledged or acted upon, but the mere writing of it served to strengthen my backbone and cement my resolve.

It wasn't until junior high that beauty-based cliques began forming between girls, and sports bonding began between boys. While holding daily court in the cafeteria at lunchtime, most of them entertained each other by taunting their rejects. One gym teacher, enjoying camaraderie with parents of the offenders, demonstrated her allegiance by further embarrassing students targeted by the cliques. In addition to assigning them extra laps and locker room duty, she openly scorned their abilities and detained them for fabricated infractions. The first day she aimed her mockery at me, I left class and never returned.

Years later, on the afternoon of the Honors Assembly when I was to graduate as the student with the most curricular earned medals pinned to her robe, my class counselor called me in for a conference.

"Your records indicate you failed gym for six years running," he said.

"I didn't fail. I didn't attend."

"Then you can't graduate until you do."

"So, you're suggesting I go to summer school for swimming, softball, basketball, and badminton?"

Needless to say, I graduated. He changed my records from failing to passing to make that possible, inadvertently raising my overall grade point average.

Bullying wasn't as effective in senior high due to the size of the campus and larger student population. Instead, a parent's place in the hierarchy of city society coerced choices for cheerleading, club leadership, school government, and homecoming participation. And, while the number of menacing teachers was fewer, their presence remained.

When a homeroom student became pregnant and was expelled (because that's how unwed motherhood was handled in the sixties), my English teacher forbade all her students from speaking to her. Nevertheless, when I spotted her clearing out her locker, I walked over to say goodbye. Someone tattled. As punishment, I received a D in English. But it evened out. To counter the underserved D, I earned a well-deserved A in journalism, prompting the principal to nominate me for editor of the school newspaper and the school board selecting me, unanimously.

I'm convinced that school bullies become business bullies, and many of their victims 'follow the leader' as adults.

After moving to New York, I witnessed an art department director harass employees by declaring his completion of a single college psychology course qualified him to assail their incompetence; a merchandising manager who blamed his mistakes on clerks to the point of him falsifying production documents; the head of a security firm who goaded employees on vacation by phoning them to demand they solve nonexistent problems. The list is long. It demonstrates how those who feel compelled to think, speak, or act in a manner not of their choosing continue to be bullied throughout life, in some manner, by someone.

· · ·

Since 1976, I've earned my living as an entrepreneur, writer, and designer. I'd like to say it makes me bullied-free. Alas, that's impossible for anyone to truthfully claim. Between friends, relatives, colleagues, employers, government agencies, consumer services, business organizations, clubs, neighborhood associations, naysayers, politicians, reporters, social media, talking heads, telemarketers, contractors, zealots, line jumpers, road rage and the rest, we *all* encounter daily degrees of bullying.

So let's stop telling kids that bullies are a schoolroom problem graduation solves, or law enforcement can control, or Congress can legislate against.

It's time we begin addressing the very fabric of our society that suffers bullying as a way of life we indulge in and enable as an expedient means to our tentative survival. Only then can we stand up as a nation and demand that bullies (of all ages, in all areas, at all levels) stand down.

Because tormentors can't be conquered by timidity.

It takes courage.

It demands virtue.

It requires an ethical resolve by us all.

# # #

## 8

IT COULD HAPPEN TO YOU, TOO

*W*ere I to write my epitaph, it would read, "She lived a charmed life." Those who have only known *of* me might not agree — but those who've known me well, would. Consider this as evidence of that.

August often stifles New York, much like it did forty-six years ago, with temperatures so high and rain so scarce a brownout swept over all five boroughs, leaving the city sweltering in virtual darkness from dusk until dawn.

We were living in Bensonhurst, renting the upper two floors of a 1925 three-story duplex — a fort-like house located on a tree-lined street not far from a rumored underboss residence. It was a neighborhood where no one locked their doors at night, and old-country madonnas garbed in basic-black sat in fold-out lawn chairs on cement sidewalks, waiting for the intense fragrances of Sicilian sausage, fennel seed biscotti, and basil-based sauces to waft through their kitchen windows, signaling meals had simmered to perfection and were ready for serving.

Our home's private entrance had four steps up to the front door. Once inside, there were another seven steps up to the hallway landing leading to a bedroom, living room, dining room, and bathroom, with a second flight of stairs to two more bedrooms. A doorway leading off the dining room opened to an eat-in kitchen. Another opened from the living room onto a second-floor veranda stretching 25 feet long and 15 feet deep, with a 4-foot high wall leveling off just below the treetops.

We loved that place and porch, especially in August when sleeping outside beat the heat of the house by thirty degrees, and the starlit sky with its Creamsicle moon overhead was about as romantic as any heart could wish for or mind could imagine.

It was after ten one night when we were out there, lying on army surplus canvas and wood framed cots, listening to the neighbors battery-operated radios synchronized to Casey Kasem naming "And I Love You So" by America's favorite barber holding at #38 on the Top 40 charts when we heard a knock on the door.

Liz called out, "Who's there?"

"I'm looking for Marge," came a baritone response.

"Who are you?"

"Mike Kelly."

"Are you Irish?"

"I am."

"Then the door's open. Come on up."

.   .   .

At the time, I was incapacitated from being hit by a drunk driver that left me chronically disabled months earlier. As predicted, I'd regained my ability to walk, but still needed a wheelchair, or walker on occasion, and would come to need a cane, always. As I struggled up and into a lightweight summer robe, Liz donned hers and greeted the fellow with our Coleman lantern in tow, leading him out onto the porch and offering him a seat at the fold-out card table stationed there for Canasta and Hearts competitions. Then she excused herself to get us all some bagged iced lemonade while I tried to read his face by the street lamp.

I liked what I saw. Mike Kelly had a crinkle-eyed smile plastered to his super-sized mug, with a pencil mustache complementing his noggin of silky gray hair.

"I'm sorry to bother you so late," he began, "but you never contacted us. I had to take the Long Island Railroad from Port Washington after work and two subways — then got lost while walking here from the El."

"Why should I have contacted you, Mr. Kelly?"

"Mike, please."

"Mike."

"Didn't you get our telegram about winning Publisher's Clearing House?"

I laughed out loud. "Come now, Mikey. You can do better. Although, I must admit, I've never heard that line before."

He grinned. "Darn. I wish I'd thought of it before I got too old and too happily married for come-ons to matter anymore."

"What's so funny," Liz chimed in, sliding a tin tray of refreshments onto the table.

"I was just telling Mike here about my last encounter with

Publisher's Clearing House."

"You had one?" Mike asked.

"Sort of. While I was partially paralyzed, I passed the time by answering those ridiculous Cosmos questionnaires before playing wastebasket wad-ball. I confess. One of the wads was a Publishers Clearing House entry."

"She'd ordered a photography and a camping magazine," added Liz.

"True, but I figured I'd never be going camping again, and wouldn't be anywhere interesting to shoot photographs for a long while — so I wadded it up and made the basket."

"Well, that explains it," chuckled Mike.

"What?"

"Your wrinkled entry."

"But I didn't…"

"I did," Liz interjected. We both turned toward her. "I took it out of the wastebasket and smoothed it out the best I could and mailed it in. Whenever a magazine came in the mail, I hid it. I thought I'd give them all to you on your birthday. I guess I was hoping, by then, maybe, you'd feel like camping and taking pictures again." Her words turned maudlin inside me.

Mike Kelly beamed. "This is where I tell you — *again* — you've won Publisher's Clearing House."

I'll end this on that high note — but not because there isn't more to tell about the trip around Manhattan included with the monetary prize, our suite at the Waldorf Astoria, the nights on the town, dinner at the Rainbow Room, orchestra seats to *A Little Night Music*, the yacht ride to Port Washington,

the catered brunch, a tour of the PCH facility, the awards ceremony, the photographer and limousine at our disposal for the
weekend, the parties, the clubs we closed, the Jim Bailey meet
and greet in the Empire Room at the hotel, the new friends
made, the fun, and the fanfare. It's more because — you really
had to be there — and I'd rather not ruin the surprise.

The following year, I agreed to make the first televised
commercial for PCH. It ran between 11:30 a.m. and 11:30 p.m.
on all three of the only major networks back then. If you were
watching television in December of 1974 and saw a news
program, soap opera, game show, sports event, or family
favorite like *The Rockford Files*, *The Waltons*, *Kojak*, *Medical
Center*, *Mash*, and *Chico & The Man* — yep. That was me saying
it could happen to you, too.

There's no drawback to the entire Publisher's Clearing
House experience except in one, small respect, and that is —
no matter what I've done with my life, who I am, where I live,
whom I love, what I've accomplished, or contributed — it
seems like each time I meet those from my very distant past,
the first thing they mention is that I won Publisher's Clearing
House, followed by the implication that my life has been "easy"
because of it.

And I always let it pass.

Because — even though it was only the mystery prize of
$17,500 and all of it went to pay off past-due medical bills — I
know.

I've led a charmed life.

# # #

## 9

PANTS ON FIRE

I've been editing answers to my partner about something-or-other for 45 years. I consider it a key ingredient in the recipe of happily ever after.

Oh sure, I know honesty has been touted as imperative between couples for centuries, and good books will be thumped in outrage at me for being an avowed fabricator.

No matter.

I maintain that the best way to stay hopelessly devoted is to — subjectively and selectively — fib.

Let's start with her terrible twos. Regardless of the fact that my much better half has enough clothes to restock the shelves of a small boutique, she doesn't wear 85% of her wardrobe. Instead, day in and out she dons the same outfits for an average of two years running because each shirt, pair of slacks, sweater, sweatshirt, pajama top, tee, and jacket on a revolving variety rack of two garments per category is proclaimed to be her "favorite."

This is where bleach becomes my buddy. I accidentally splash bleach, or spill bleach, or mistake a spray bottle of Soft Scrub for Shout, or add Clorox instead of fabric softener to the rinse-cycle of any garment (including my own) that I cannot bear looking at for a tub-of-water longer. In fact, hearing her scream from the laundry room "You idiot!" is like music to my ears and victory to my eyes.

Saving her from potential harm is a constant, like when she insists it's safe to clean the car mats placed on the ground during the pouring rain because she's using a dry/wet vacuum. Combating this and other latent disasters require falsifying. That's where being a commercial artist comes in handy. Almost all interviews written about her favorite celebrities can be altered to reflect safer choices before being printed out, complete with stock photos. It gives me comfort to know she listens to the tweaked advice of long-gone megastars. (Bless their little borrowed hearts.)

There was a time when too many kitchen tools presented a challenge because she can't accept the fact that every good cook has her own set of knives, knowing the size, weight, and feel of each in her hand, its purpose and degree of sharpness for meat, vegetable, bread, or bone.

But my dearheart has a dire need to buy every plastic handled five-and-dime knife at garage sales that "look just like" my wood handled German and Japanese cutlery. (They don't. Not even close.)

My solution was to fill a small kitchen drawer with her knockoffs. Now, every time she comes home with a knife, I act excited, steal a kiss and quietly deposit the knife in the garbage. If she asks about the newbies, I point her toward the drawer.

Speaking of vegetables (as in overbuying them), that's what the lidded bowl on my Kitchen Aide mixer hides. So far, the neighbors haven't figured out who leaves fresh veggies in alternating mailboxes late at night, but none have complained, either.

Except for her. "I wish someone would leave *us* free tomatoes in our mailbox," she's said. "How come we never get left a Chiquita?" she's asked. "The fruit fairy must not like you," she's decided.

"Me?" I dare. "Not you?"

"Don't be silly. *Everyone* likes me."

That's true. But in fairness, I did once sneak a Macintosh apple into our mailbox. She bemoaned that it wasn't a Pink Lady.

Inanimate objects are also factored in. Semiannually, she'll want tickets to an Oldies But Goodies concert advertised weeks in advance of the event. I'll squeeze her hand, promise we'll go, and hurry off to write the concert on the calendar as a reminder before returning to her with a treat — a dish of ice cream, cookie, popcorn, or such. But I never actually record the event because she invariably forgets that it only took our attending one of those dreadful $40 per ticket concerts to teach me to ... well ... edit.

And so it goes.

Personally, I don't understand those who always need to be right when an argument erupts, or prove a point, or stand on principle, or choose to hold others to a higher standard of truthfulness than they practice themselves, or insist that communication is the key to a good marriage.

Because, while she and I are seldom diametrically opposed on any important issue, if she isn't going to budge, I'll always acquiesce. I'm convinced that — unless conversation is salted with sincerity, peppered with levity, and garnished with good intentions — it isn't communication at all.

It's babel.

That being said, I must confess I wasn't being honest when I wrote, "I've been editing answers to my partner about some-thing-or-other for 45 years."

It's actually been 49 years.

And that's the truth.

# # #

## 10

LADY LUCK

I'm not a superstitious person by nature. I don't think of black cats or the number 13 as unlucky. I don't knock on wood to ensure things go well. When my right eye twitches, I don't believe there'll be a birth in the family. And if a candle suddenly blows out, I'm certain it doesn't signal spirits will come calling.

Except (maybe) sometimes.

Because something so *bizarre* befell us one long ago Halloween night, people have been brushing the residue of salt off my left shoulder ever since.

It happened up north in a time when the holiday was still animated via those moms who made scrap cloth costumes for their kids and let them run unassisted through neighborhoods where every house had someone eager to marvel over foil-winged angels, chicken-feathered fairies, eye-patch pirates, sheeted ghosts, and comic heroes in tinted tights wearing scarlet skivvies and pillowcase capes.

Liz and I had just such a home that omened October, numbered 13 Cheshire Street, set back on a cul-de-sac with its vintage wraparound casement porch facing north and attached deck laundry facing south.

Why we'd decorated both entries that year remains baffling, but we did, with every accordion-style paper ghost and goblin we could find at Woolworth's. We tied dried corn-stalks around the doors and scattered straw over the floors. The sidewalks were lined with jack-o-lanterns lit by three-inch Sabbath candles. A witch's silhouette swayed on the front door with tiny plastic bats dangling from her broomstick. A black cat cutout hung on the back door over a *Scat!* sign scrib-bled especially for the occasion.

Inside, candied and caramelized apples, pink popcorn balls, teal blue bubble gum cigars, white powdered donuts and warmed cider in fold-out handle paper cups were arranged on a long linen-clothed table, free for the glee of anticipated trick-or-treaters.

Who never came. Nary a one.

Instead, a moonless, tempestuous, indigo sky of four winds, spewing sleet descended, making mayhem before depositing a gravestone cold in its wake.

Wiser women would have felt a sense of foreboding. We just went to bed.

"Wake me when it's over," Liz said, dispirited. "And not a second sooner."

Around midnight I heard howling, intermittent at first, but gradually growing into a wail. I slipped out of bed and felt a shudder when opening the window to spot a solitary candle still flickering within a collapsed black-frosted pumpkin. Soon, that lone light in the night died.

"Power's just out," I whispered to myself while creeping blindly down the stairs and through the house to the kitchen where I felt around to find a flashlight, ever fearful of the steady, doleful crying.

Nevertheless, I unlocked the kitchen door leading into the laundry room, then mustered up the courage to cautiously crack open its backyard door, illuminating the deck steps.

There sat a black cat yowling through quivering whiskers.

"You're quite the screamer," I hushed, ushering him in.

After wrapping the cat in a towel grabbed from the hamper, I fashioned a bed from some leftover straw, placing it and him inside the dryer before cracking the door and returning to bed.

At half-past four, the caterwauling began again. This time, a flashing clock dial signaled the power was restored. Exhausted, I staggered up and stumbled down to the deck door, only to find Liz had put the screamer back outside.

"She must have mistaken your cries as nature calling," I minimized to the cat while scooping him up and smuggling him to the basement where I hid him in a corrugated box filled with my best cotton rags. During my sleep-stumble back to bed, I fashioned the reprimand I planned to give Liz for her indefensible bad behavior.

The scolding wasn't to be. Well-rested and up early, Liz was already at the sink making coffee when I hurried past her heading down the basement stairs, shocked to find the screamer not a 'him' but a 'her,' smug as a bug in a hug while nursing six newborn kittens.

"Egad, I'm in for it now!" I surmised, way-*way* too loud.

"In for what?" Liz called back.

I didn't answer. I couldn't. Instead, I sheepishly carted the box of kittens up to the kitchen with momma cat in tow. "Wait until you see what I've found in the basement," I ventured.

But by then Liz was hunting dish towels in the laundry, yelling, "What's this cat doing in our clothes dryer?"

I froze. "Cat?" I asked — you know, all innocent-like.

"Cats!" she replied. "A black cat with five kittens."

So, there you have it. Do the math. Thirteen cats came calling in the span of one Halloween night, half of them pitch black, and the rest of them might as well have been.

Because we kept them. All.

It was just my luck.

# # #

This refreshed essay copyrighted by Marguerite Quantaine © 2011 first appeared in Kissed By Venus Magazine.

AN INCONVENIENT PINK

*J*f I kept a book of regrets, my first entry would be that I failed to appreciate the wedding dress my mom made for herself. She took such pride in it. She loved it so.

Mom appeared and acted younger than her 93 years when her eyes took a sudden drift toward blindness, her uncanny ability to hear whispered conversations of those across the room faded, and a fall the year earlier demanded she could no longer live alone in the town of her birth and lifelong residency. It broke her spirit to leave her home, her two elder cats, and most of her belongings behind during an acquiescence to my sister Susan's Texas ranch those last months of her life.

Among the few garments she'd wrapped and packed with care was her pale pink wedding dress of 1938 that she learned to make in intermediate school more than a decade earlier. I can't say if Mom intended for Sue, me, or our kid sister, Kate, to someday wear her wedding gown, but I do know Kate and I had already declared by age eight that neither of us ever intended to marry. And it might have been equally disheartening (if not embarrassing) for Mom when all three of her daughters so disdained Home Economics in school that none of us finished hemming even one dish towel to the satisfaction of Miss Merriman, the same teacher who'd first taught Mom to sew.

Nevertheless, I felt honored to be both Mom's namesake and heir to her love for the color pink, a pigment that looked best on her and always brings out the best in me. In fact, I seldom wear any other color, feeling more poised when I do.

Mom wasn't as obsessed with the color as am I, she being more of a fashionista whenever she left the house. Her outfits always included a splash of pink in a hair ornament, a bangle on her wrist, beads around her neck, a porcelain broach, or a cloth flower pinned near her heart.

Years ago, as I sat with sister Kate discussing Mom's passing, she unpacked the wedding gown and conferred it to me for safer keeping. Upon tenderly removing it from its bed of tissue, I marveled — "It's exquisite."

Unlike modern gowns that average fifteen hundred dollars in apparel stores and run higher than ten thousand in bridal boutiques, Mom's dress was an innocent, ultra-sheer Heberlein organdy acclaimed for crispness, yet as light as gossamer. The pastel pink fabric, embroidered with rows of one-inch white flowers separated by rows of half-inch white petals and stems, was perfectly cut as a single piece floor length gown. Its mirrored left fold was cleverly creased and sewn up the right side in matching pink thread. There were tiny hidden snaps under the arms, a flounce encircling the knee above the

A-flared skirt, and puffy sleeves framing a single notch neckline.

"I'm ashamed to say I spent six years as a production control manager in New York City's garment industry purchasing piece goods and dealing with jobbers, cutters, designers, and sewers daily — yet never once, Kate, did I think to appreciate this dress made by Mom."

"Yeah. Well. That's true. But it *is* a wedding gown, after all. Why would we?"

"Still. The innovativeness and pure, perfect intricacy of it blows me away. And that she chose pink! How audacious."

"I don't follow."

"You know, it being 1938 and all. She went against the catwalk code of wearing white."

"That would be you, not her."

"I get it from her."

"But it's not why she wore pink."

I gazed up from the gown, puzzled. "No? Why then?"

"She'd been married before."

Her answer stunned me. "Mom was married before Dad?"

"Uh-huh."

"You knew?"

"We all knew."

"All being...?"

"The rest of the family."

"Have you known for long?"

"No." She stopped to think. "Only about forty years. Maybe fifty."

I sat, locked in a blank stare, feeling flabbergasted. "How come no one ever told me?"

Kate shrugged. "You've always seen Mom through rose-colored glasses. I wasn't about to cloud them. Besides, it's not as if we ever discussed it once we knew."

Within weeks, I'd found her first husband's name, date of birth and death, military record, marriage license, divorce decree with the listed grounds, burial place and downloaded a picture of his tombstone. I'm still searching for his face, convinced that every writer's DNA includes a need-to-know-the-ending to a story.

But wasn't she brave? I thought through the research of it all. *To marry and divorce and demand the court restore the legitimacy of her maiden name during a period of time when valiant women were demonized, and divorcées were treated as pariahs?*

Mom.

I took such pride in her.

I loved her so.

\# \# \#

CRUSH 101

*D*eatsville wasn't any bigger than a whistle and a walk in 1954, about as far due south of my Michigan birthplace as any eight year old could imagine. The roads running east and west past Popeye's two-pump, glass-globe gasoline stop-and-shop had the soft, dust-rusty look of a boiled bare five-and-dime enamelware pan.

I'd traveled to Deatsville to spend the summer with my cohort, Molly, and her parents who owned that screen door gathering spot frequented mostly by natives of Elmore County and day trippers from Lomax and Verbena who'd gotten side-tracked on their way to Montgomery.

Molly and I were counterfeit cousins, joined at the heart and mind's eye instead of the kinsman hip. Our mommas had been best friends before us. They'd met in New York City where each had fled during the 1930s, intent on finding a more sophisticated lifestyle than that of a small-town girl grown into a small-town wife. Marriage and children returned them to convention, but our births had awarded each a vicarious second chance at adventure.

In time, we'd give them some of their dreams, but for that last unadulterated summer of our youth, we were as any other children growing up in the kind of rural community that red line roads on paper pocket maps connected.

"Do as you're told and make me proud," was my mother's marching order. (I did and would.)

I arrived by bus, the driver making a stop at Popeye's even though it wasn't on his scheduled route. Had he chosen to obey orders to pass by Deatsville, visitors and residents of the area would have had to find additional transportation back to there. Stopping was the common southern courtesy that northern dispatchers were forced to either accept or ignore.

Molly and her dog, Buford, greeted me by dancing barefoot in the dirt, a piece of her momma's pecan pie held high in her right hand while she wigwagged the left.

"Hi, *you all*," she enunciated with an exaggerated drawl.

I kissed her. Then I bent down and kissed Buford before kissing the pie.

"I ate mine already, but you can share yours with me if you want," she hinted.

We slept in a tall-walled room at the end of a tongue-and-groove hallway of a 19th-century carpetbaggers house set five hundred feet back from the store. It was a proud, old, chipped-paint clapboard structure with faded green plantation shutters hiding nine foot, nine-over-nine pane windows, most of them swollen shut. Those that worked opened like doors onto wraparound porches connecting pencil post pillars to a sloping tin roof that provided both shade and shelter from the relentless heat and sudden white rains of an Alabama afternoon.

"I've got a secret to show you," Molly whispered one afternoon while we feigned napping. Together we crawled under her grandma's iron bed and removed the floorboards to an inwardly opening trap door exposing a ladder that took us ten feet down into a somber cellar of red clay and hollowed out slots where candles once burned as lighting.

"Wow," I awed, gleefully.

"I dug this hole for you," she lied, believing I believed her.

It was into this pit that Molly and I dragged all the comforts of home — two stools, my teddy bear, pillows and blankets, more yahrzeit candles, Crayolas, Little Lulu comic books, Ball jars of water, Ritz crackers, peanut butter, wood stick matches, and the very latest communication system Molly found detailed on a Bazooka bubble gum wrapper calling for the connecting of two empty Campbell's soup cans with a kite string that, when pulled tightly and talked into, would transmit our voices through the cord. Never mind that we were inseparable, so there would never be anyone at the other end of the line tied uselessly to the bedpost overhead.

We spent most of the summer in that hole while her parents thought we were elsewhere doing who-knew-what. But come the end of August, her folks decided to close up shop and take us to visit kin in Montgomery.

I don't recall anything good about that trip because it rained daily, and we were confined to the commands and prickly scrutiny of distantly related adults. But I do remember returning to Deatsville the first sunny day after the deluge to discover Molly's home had been swallowed by a sinkhole the size of a city block, taking the tale of our secret space with it.

Once summer ended, I was suddenly back in Michigan meeting my third-grade teacher, Miss Grimmel, on the opening day of school. She had thick auburn hair tied tightly in a bun behind her head, brown eyes wider than walnuts, scarlet lipstick, the whitest teeth, and connect-the-dots freckles on every uncovered inch of her paste-pale face, arms, legs, and hands. I spent my school days mesmerized by her and eager to please.

Although, I never saw my imaginary friend, Molly, again, that long ago September-to-February-memory of Miss Grimmel endures with clarity. Her black horned-rim glasses straddling an arrowy nose, the low pitch of her voice, the faint fragrance of violet cologne following her up and down the aisles and the stern look she gave anyone tempted to act up.

Some sixty-five years and many thousands of miles since, I still have the Valentine's Day card she sent to me by first-class mail, arriving a week after the morning the principal informed our class that Miss Grimmel had eloped, left town, and would no longer be our teacher.

It soothed my broken heart.

# # #

MY DAY OF DALLYING

I'm sitting in my office at Fuller & Smith & Ross on the 36th floor of a forty-one story Fifth Avenue Manhattan skyscraper known as the Top of the Sixes. It's the summer of 1967, shortly before our advertising agency's media acumen is chosen to put Richard Nixon into the White House.

I've been working here since 1965 when I was hired as a lowly media clerk for several months before skyrocketing up the ladder to become the Manager of Purchasing, Interiors, & In-House Printing. I'm listed as an executive because this is FSR's corporate headquarters with branch offices in Cleveland, Chicago, San Francisco, and Los Angeles.

That sounds like I should be sophisticated, but I'm not — not by any stretch of my imagination no matter how well I dress. Instead, I'm 21 going on 35 professionally, but am otherwise unworldly.

I've met each employee on the two floors occupied by FSR

because they've all been in need of office necessities in the course of doing their jobs, and I've made a protocol of personal delivery to everyone except to Mr. Mahoney, the Senior Vice-President Creative Director, whom I've only seen once, in passing, as he exited an elevator leaving a pungent waft of Christian Dior's Eau Sauvage in his wake. We've not yet met because he's never requested anything.

Until this morning.

"Hello, purchasing, Margie speaking. How…"

"Bring me a Dixon Ticonderoga #2 pencil at once."

"With whom am I having the pleasure of…"

"Mr. Mahoney." Click.

I suspect the demand is a ploy to get me behind closed doors. My wonder is, why?

Mr. Mahoney is as dapper as Cary Grant, seemingly as tall, but not nearly as handsome. He has thick, perfectly styled and parted Vitalis-laden silver hair and meticulously manicured hands. He's a nasal sounding enunciator who (I'm told) was schooled and bred in old money and groomed as an elitist gentleman. Although married with children, his detractors disparage him as being light in the loafers.

His office is locked behind perpetually closed doors on the south side of the building with windows that would have overlooked East 52nd Avenue and Schraft's Restaurant if he hadn't had them paneled over to create a chamber of solitude and quietude.

"Come in," he answers to my almost inaudible tap, "and close the door behind you."

I do and am instantly taken aback.

The room is pitch black except for Mr. Mahoney sitting in a George Mulhauser molded chair behind the twelve-foot-long, custom-made, Giuseppe Scapinelli Jacaranda wood desk I recognize from admiring examples of in catalogs and at trade shows. But it's the painting illuminated on the wall, inches above and behind him that renders me both mute and motionless.

The oil on canvas measures maybe four feet high by exactly as long as the desk. At first, it appears to be a variant of *St. John of the Cross*, cropped just below St. John's bowed head and just above his spiked hands, framed at the very edge of the wood cross blending into the painting's narrow slat frame.

Except it's not actually the *St. John of the Cross* but the spiked, bleeding crown of what resembles Jesus Christ with the bowed top head in the painting centered perfectly above the head of Mr. Mahoney.

"What do you think?" a voice from the darkness asks.

"I'm not sure," I stammer. "It's like my eyes are glued to it. I can't seem to move."

"You were right," speaks the voice to him.

"You're excused," says Mr. Mahoney to me.

In pivoting to leave, I see the faint outline of a man in a cauliflower white vested suit and Havana hat sitting with his legs crossed on a couch against the back wall. He's otherwise invisible until I open the door to a light streaming in from the hallway. I glance over to notice how pale his face is, and how pretentious his long, skinny, black waxed twisted upwards mustache appears. He's eerily exotic.

I'll never again see the painting, either in a photograph, or coffee table book, or art catalog, or hanging elsewhere.

But I do see the man in the cauliflower suit later that day. He's standing alone in Paley Park, admiring the waterfall. I'm there to buy a cup of coffee from the concessionaire, but instead, I spend my time leaning against a honey locust tree, watching the man watching the water.

# # #

SEE YA LATER, ALLIGATOR

The first time I spotted an alligator in the murky waters of a man-made lake framing luxurious condos on one side and a city park on the other, I worried aloud for the safety of the mallards, Muscovy, white waddling ducks, snapping turtles, giant goldfish, flocks of pristine egrets and wading blue herons making their homes in the marshes there.

"And the kids who play in this park," my sweetheart added.

I didn't respond. Not that I would ever want a person of any age to be harmed by an alligator, but there was no imminent danger in that. Only nature-preying-nature lurked.

The faux lake is more for show-and-tell by realtors looking to justify pricey units with a view. There's no swimming allowed, and since it's illegal to feed wildlife in Florida outside of a reserve, observing nature in this park is mostly done from a deck built 15 feet above, and stretching 20 feet out over the water on which picnic tables are placed for brown baggers wondering what so many thieving seagulls are doing perched there, some sixty miles inland.

At first, all I saw were the mammoth marble shaped alligator eyes trolling the lake's surface, leaving innocent ripples of water in his wake.

"Or," she said when I pointed out the marauder, "it's a submarine."

"No, hon, I'm pretty certain it's an alligator."

"But I'm thinking, if…"

"It's a *gator*, okay?"

"I'm just saying what it could be," she persisted as the tire-like tracks on its back emerged. "Or maybe one in camouflage to look like an alligator so no one would suspect."

Really, who am I to insist otherwise? I thought. *We only visit this particular park once a year, in September or October, depending on what date the High Holy Days fall.*

I won't expound on the significance of these ten days for those of you who aren't Jewish, but I will share the custom of *tashlikh*, the casting of bread upon the water as a symbol of one's transgressions being disposed of. Unlike other religions, Jews don't believe in original sin. Instead, we're born pure, acquiring our indiscretions with age, intent, or ignorance along the way.

However, if we're sincere in saying "I'm sorry" to those we've wronged, done good without expectation in return, and made an earnest effort to mend fences, the sin slate gets wiped clean on Yom Kippur giving each of us another chance to get life right and do it better.

The disclaimer appears in the setting of the sun symbolizing the closing of the Book of Life when even skeptics hope theirs and the names of their loved ones are inscribed therein. And since only those remaining in the here-and-now know who was inscribed back in the then-and-there, no one learns if they made the cut until the High Holy Days roll around again the following year.

For the record, I'm very disorganized about organized religion to the point of being anti-it. But I do relish Rosh Hashanah and Yom Kippur, the culmination of ten days of introspection, taking stock of one's life, offering amends, being grateful for whatever cards have been dealt, making promises, and looking forward while witnessing the sun sink behind the trees, or beneath the ocean, or into the hills.

Of course, I'm pulling for more than family and friends. I want my pets to be included in that Book of Life, too, and mercy shown for all the animals on earth. I want children to be protected and hurts healed. I want every woman to fall in love with the person who has fallen in love with her. My list is long. I ask a lot. It takes me the full ten days to catalog all the hope in my heart.

"Watch out," we were warned by a couple dawdling nearby. "The flora and fauna police are on duty."

I glance over at the retiree in khaki shirt and shorts, feeling powerful on his unpaid patrol.

"I'm prepared," I assured them. "I filled my pocket with stale, pre-pulverized bread to melt any evidence upon impact. Would you like some?"

They showed me their cut-up crusts of challah. "No thanks. We're good."

As the sun began its steady decline, I confidently hurled a handful of crumbs to flutter like tiny confetti into the water below — forgetting that the brass ring containing the keys to the car, our home, my sister's home, the metal license tags of our dogs, and a silver kitty charm carried for good luck was also in that pocket. It went with.

"I'll be," she said, looking down at the unintended snack. "It *is* an alligator!"

To paraphrase a verse in a song from the original Broadway cast album of *The Unsinkable Molly Brown*: "Your prayer was answered, the answer was *no*. She heard you all right."

Many of those who've friended me on Facebook know that we lost my kid sister in May of 2015, 77 days after she was first diagnosed with everywhere-cancer. What I haven't shared as much is, during the weeks directly after her passing, we also lost both of our dogs, our Siamese, and our Russian Blue cat to very old age.

When the last of the losses happened, I recalled some words attributed to Virginia Woolf. Upon being asked by her niece why the bird she'd found had to die, Woolf answered, "To make us appreciate life more."

I'm not sure I agree. I don't think I could appreciate life any more than I do. My gratitude is fierce and immense and never falters — even when the answer is, assuredly, no. Because I see, hear, and recognize the loss many others endure, daily, is so much greater than my own; the worldwide despair and hunger of millions in the dark of every night, the destruction of homes by flood and fire, the assault on nature by ignorance and greed, the ongoing slaughter of innocent and innocence, the intentional harm inflicted on the undeserving.

It doesn't lessen the depth of loss I feel — but it does lessen the length of time I spend struggling.

The High Holy Days come earlier this year, and I'm on tenterhooks about it to the point of being mindful of the fact that the ritual of *tashlikh* is to happen on the second day of Rosh Hashanah, *not* on Yom Kippur as I've always chosen to observe it.

We'll return to the man-made lake, regardless, this time with an entire loaf of challah for the alligator.

We hope the reptile was written into the Book of Life.

We hope we *all* were.

# # #

COLD CASE

*I*n 1959 I knew a girl who, like me, aspired to be a writer. Her name was Ann. She was an oddity of sorts among the girls I occasionally accompanied to Brown's Pharmacy where we sat at the counter on hot summer afternoons and ate Cheese Doodles while sipping Cokes through waxed paper straws in glasses topped off with half-inch ice cubes.

At five-foot-one, weighing not quite eighty pounds, I was a wisp. Ann was taller by several inches and heavier, with a pronounced pear-shaped body. Although her family appeared prominent by living in a big house in a better neighborhood, Ann dressed in drab colors, had rhinestone studded wing shaped eyeglasses that she constantly shoved up to the top of her exposed wide nostril nose, wore shiny steel braces on her teeth, and fixed her dark brown flyaway hair in an unflattering under-curled bob connected at the forehead by bangs.

But Ann was smart and witty and made me laugh.

We'd both turned thirteen in '59 (on a maturity scale closer to eight by Millennials standards) and were as innocent as the hits of Brenda Lee, Del Shannon, Connie Francis, and Dion sounded on the radio, or *Leave It To Beaver*, *Father Knows Best*, and *The Patty Duke Show* depicted on the tube. Girls wore hoop skirts over crinolines or dresses to school with knee highs or bobby socks. Dinners were served at six, nobody smoked or swore in public, and subjects of a carnal nature weren't open for discussion.

When the 20th anniversary celebrating *Gone With The Wind* came to town that year, Ann and I went to a matinee together, sitting in the front row of the balcony at the downtown Michigan theater.

Enthralled by the majesty of the production and enchanted by the war correspondence exchanged between Scarlett O'Hara and Ashley Wilkes, we decided the best way to hone our writing skills would be to challenge each other by pretending to be Scarlett writing letters to Ashley.

We did this by my purchasing a small brown notebook of lined paper in which Ann, as Scarlett, would pen a love letter to Ashley, and give it to me as a challenge. I'd try to out-write her by following course. We would hand this booklet back and forth from day to day, each one allowed the evening after school to compose a new letter to Ashley from Scarlett.

The notebook and those words we wrote are now long gone and forgotten, but nothing we penned was vulgar or suggestive. Neither of us understood the intimacies of love, the innuendo of scenes seen on the screen, nor the true definition of unseemly words at the time. It was simply a game of pretend.

This exchange went on until a week before our first day of ninth grade. That's when Ann informed me her mother said she could no longer associate with me in any manner, anywhere, at any time.

"Can I have the notebook back?" I asked.

"My mom burned it."

I assumed our friendship ended because her parents were wealthier than mine and members of the country club set, or because Ann always buttoned her blouses at the top and I didn't, or because I was color coordinated, or she was Methodist, or they didn't want her becoming a writer. But it never occurred to me that her mother interpreted the innocence of our words as perverse.

I would tell you that I was distraught by the loss of Ann's friendship and the four years of meanness from other classmates and several teachers that followed — but I wasn't. Because I didn't know that Ann had been told I was queer, and I didn't know Ann told all our mutual friends her mother said I was queer, and I didn't know her mother told the parents of mutual friends I was queer, and I didn't know certain teachers were warned of the same.

In fact, I didn't even know the word 'queer' meant anything other than unconventional and curious. (I've always been both of those.)

Nevertheless, over time and in retrospect, I came to wonder why another student had written "queer" in two places in my 9th grade yearbook for all the other students to read. It must have been disappointing that I never seemed fazed by the queer tag connected to me by that clique of classmates and group of teachers. But how could they know, the primary reason I never accepted party invitations, or attended sports events, or showed up at school dances was because, by age fourteen, I'd forged my folks names to a work permit so I could take a job from 4 to 9, five nights a week, and 9 to 9 on Saturdays?

All that hatred shot to hell on an impervious target.

Five years after my high school graduation, and never having had a crush on anyone other than my third-grade teacher, never having had a steady friend, never having had an intimate relationship of any kind with any gender, and (subsequently) never having had my heart broken — I looked across a crowded room and fell instantly in love with the woman looking back at me.

Fast forward to 2014.

Upon checking my emails, I found one from someone who'd attended my 50th high school reunion, thirteen hundred miles away. Like all such reunions before, the occasion had come and gone without me in attendance.

The email proved part apology and part confession for having heard of the brown book and being complicit in the mocking, backstabbing, and shunning while remaining silent, even to the snide remarks made at the reunion of "have you heard" and "I told you so" from those who've never known squat.

Well, well, well, I thought. *Isn't that something? After all these years, a cold case solved.*

But here's an epilogue, nonetheless:

Entire worlds exist of just two people in love. I've now been wildly-so for the same person who's been wildly-so for me these 49 years. We've experienced the most amazing, wonderful, exciting, diverse, productive, resourceful, creative, meaningful, successful, charmed and utterly joyful life together. Even the adversities we faced were more of a breeze than a burden, and all are cherished as blessings in the scheme of things.

I would like to think we got the life we deserved.

Maybe Ann and her friends did, too.

# # #

ONLY THE NAMES HAVE CHANGED

Some stories never get old, even when tweaked over time toward truth via recently discovered records of ancestry. Such is the one about my Aunt Betty being a Michigan gun moll during the rum-running 1920s when the vast majority of illegal liquor was smuggled into the United States on boats crossing the Detroit River from Canada. As a child, I didn't know what a gun moll was, and since my ostensible relative was long gone before my birth, she remains somewhat of an enigma.

In that aspect, it's similar to the Mafia mystery of Cassie, a friendship that Elizabeth and I made after buying our home on Long Island in the mid-1970s.

During the first decade of our friendship, we didn't know Cassie was married to a goodfella. The pivotal detail only came to light after we'd accepted her invitation to join her friends aboard their yacht on Lady Liberty Day for the Statue of Liberty Centennial celebration of vessels gathering in New York Harbor on July 4th, 1986.

Perhaps we should have suspected something was amiss when the wives arrived decked out in their patriotic best for the occasion of a lifetime while their husbands donned those homogeneous black Robert Hall suits, black Wembley skinny ties, black Hanover oxfords, and black Dobb's Fedoras, all contrasted by crisp white shirts and matching white socks for partying under a midsummer sky. But it wasn't until the custom-made 44' Cabin Super Cruiser with its master state-room, two guest bedrooms, three heads, dual galleys, a dining room, and helm reception area had cast off from its berth and began racing down Long Island Sound to group-greet the largest assembly of international Tall Ships and an American armada did his capo status become evident.

The proverbial shoe dropped when Cassie's husband, Carmine, appeared on the flybridge far above the main deck where we sat happily clasping our umbrella drinks while lounging in the open console on cushioned deck chairs. We looked up to see a long line of his soldiers on the steps to his tower, waiting for an individual audience, each one honoring him by kissing the ring on his extended hand.

"Doesn't that look like a scene from *The Godfather*," Liz whispered.

"It does indeed," I agreed.

Since we had no wish to jump ship or swim with the fishes, we chose to fake fidelity by taking the hint to place our brand new Canon SureShot on a table with all the other cameras readily surrendered, then continued to drink up.

The boat ride into Manhattan was otherwise unremarkable, whereas our arrival was exhilarating. We joined 30,000 spectator crafts gathered to celebrate the centennial, setting anchor alongside the U.S.S. Sequoia Presidential Yacht. It felt momentous!

We'd only ever seen the Sequoia in photographs before then. Built in 1925, as a rich man's cruiser, it was purchased by our government in 1931 as a decoy to patrol the harbor during Prohibition when black market booze was supplied to boaters trolling the bay. Any bootlegger rowing over to sell liquor to the Sequoia was immediately arrested.

But during the final two years of his presidency, Herbert Hoover began borrowing the Sequoia from the Commerce Department to utilize it as the presidential yacht for fishing trips. It quickly became a floating White House. Over subsequent years, every other POTUS found political and pleasurable uses for the Sequoia until Jimmy Carter sold it as part of a cost-cutting campaign promise. Nonetheless, just knowing the yacht's history coupled with our being up close and personal to it was daunting.

That is, until we became sitting ducks when the anchor to the craft we were on couldn't be raised. While all other vessels quickly cleared the lane, we remained moored in the direct path of the U.S.S. John F. Kennedy, an aircraft carrier three football fields long, 192 feet high, 300 feet wide, and weighing more than 82,000 tons that began five-blasting it's horn in an effort to make us move-move-move-move-move out of harm's way as it barreled down upon us.

While Carmine struggled with the controls to avoid us being sliced and diced, not one of the 5,000 seamen standing at attention in their service dress whites on the carrier's main deck flinched. How we, along with the other thirty-one passengers on board our vessel kept calm as we donned life-jackets and fixated on the humongous ship targeted to hit us is remarkable.

In retrospect, we might have been in shock, because I can't recall any details of how Carmine got the anchor up. But I do vividly remember the yacht rocking from the bow waves hitting our accelerating stern and the quiet that blanketed us as we gradually recovered from the frightening encounter.

One thing is for certain — nobody made light of the incident, and during the following four years of our mostly-on-holidays friendship with Cassie before we moved to Florida, the centennial trip was never mentioned again.

Upon our midnight arrival to port, I went to retrieve our Canon SureShot and discovered someone had poured salt-water over it before removing the film. A week later we received a package in the mail containing photographs of us relaxing in lounge chairs aboard Cassie and Carmine's yacht. There was no return address on the envelope, no note enclosed, and no mention of my ruined camera. Not long afterward Carmine was targeted. Speculation circulated that his son carried out the hit.

The shiver of these memories made me ponder whether my Aunt Betty had any adventures of the close-call kind during her rum-runner stint as a gun moll on the Detroit River. It prompted me to email my siblings, asking what more they could add to the story of our phantom aunt.

While none of them claimed further knowledge of the gun moll account, there was talk of my grandfather being a Chicago gambler who was widowed with three very young daughters — one of them named Betty. To rectify his situation, he placed a classified ad for a mail-order bride in the *Tribune* claiming to be single and childless. Upon receiving a reply, he promptly abandoned the three little girls to a Catholic orphanage on the way to marrying my grandmother without revealing the truth to her, nor ever returning to retrieve his children.

So, technically, Betty was only my half-aunt whom my sister remembers as being the paramour of a Chicago politician, but my brother says was the mistress of the mayor of Detroit.

Whichever, her story never gets old.

# # #

SIGNING OFF

*T*he cover of my book popped up in the right-hand corner of the screen as anchor, Peter Jennings, introduced the closing story on *ABC World News Tonight* on a Friday evening in 1981. I'd authored the oversized limited run reference on the history and value of teddy bears under the Americanized spelling of my surname. It somehow engendered enough interest to garner a mention on national television.

I look back at it as pure luck now because, as any author can attest to, writing a book is often exhilarating but marketing it is *always* exhausting. In those days, it required individualized press releases being composed and printed on heavy white bond to accompany personally penned letters, each snail-mailed at considerable expense to those listed in the *Editor & Publisher Yearbook* nationwide. Even for a book as minor as mine, the effort required to sell it seemed mammoth compared to the time it took to write. That made getting featured during prime time with Peter Jennings equal to an eagle feather in a yarmulke.

The follow-up produced a headline and shout-out in the Sunday edition of *The New York Times,* not by a book reviewer, but by the much respected and often feared antiques and arts columnist, Rita Reif. I caught the wave, did some personal appearances, attended book signings, agreed to a few more interviews, and completed a stint on *PM New York* while writing a monthly column on teddies that syndicated in a dozen trade publications for several years. It was a flattering, generally enjoyable, often tiresome experience that I was grateful ended during the resurrection of teddy bear collecting among others who were tooth-and-claw dedicated to treating as their full-time endeavor. Because regardless of how glamorous it may seem or sound, that's what even minuscule fame and fleeting fortune boils down to, i.e., an eagerness and need to become the product by foregoing the person.

Fast forward to the present when everyone can be an author, cyberspace has taken over book promotion, cable and YouTube have obliterated the allure of network news, a million new books are published every year, Peter Jennings has passed away, and most periodicals containing my byline are history.

So, *thanks* for the fond memory, Peter Jennings. And may you rest in peace.

# # #

PAST, IMPERFECT, INTENSE

My father taught me things. They weren't always the right things or the best things, but he taught me all things well. One winter night while driving home alone together, he taught me about lying. I was seven.

My mom was working as a confidante and caregiver at a private cottage for forlorn cancer patients. Her curtailed quietus watch of 11 to7 promised us six kids we wouldn't awaken without her.

"I'll always be here to tuck you in and be back before breakfast," she assured. It was enough for them but not for me.

"I'm riding along," I reckoned.

"Maybe in the morning if you're up."

"Then *too*," I determined, set as cement.

She gently pressed the nub of my nose with her knuckle, lighting me up in her eyes. "You're my little lion," she said. "You give me courage."

My folks weren't friends then, if ever. Lovers once, no

doubt. He as dashing as she was beauteous. Each with ebony locks. His, glossed waves. Hers, coiled curls. His jaw, chiseled. Her cheeks, rubicund. His eyes, bruin black set tangent to an arrowed nose. Hers, bairn blue gracing a Gaelic bob. Both seeped sheen and sensuality. The two as one? An envied ornament hung among plebeians. But that was all ephemeral, lost long before the accident of me.

Oh sure, photos find him masterful in monochrome. Meritorious. Certainly indubitable. And it can be quibbled he didn't become deriding and distant until after he began colorizing her with kids. Regardless, I never espied demonstrative signs of affection between them. Neither gentility nor joy. She endured his disrespect as wifeliness while zesting motherhood. He husbanded acrimoniously, fatherly only to his firstborn.

And so it was, of all the trips we made together with mom in mind or tow, I remember that worst one best.

"Dammitall, Maggie," he one-worded her. "It's nearly eleven. Move it!"

"Don't get your bowels in an uproar," she growled back, winking my way. The dishes nearly done. The laundry almost folded. The house in chaos but cleaned down the middle and after-a-fashion. My siblings accounted for, kissed and sleeping. "I'm ready when you are."

It was the most they'd spoken to each other all day, remaining silent in their seats until he skidded to the stop where we left her just in time.

I can still envision watching her maneuver the hard packed snow and patches of ice while edging her way up the embankment toward that halfway house of enduring desperation and how my father peeled off, leaving her without help, headlights, or sentiment for her safety.

During the drive home, I kept my face glued toward the passenger window, content to imagine Mom in the morning and it being *my* nose pressed against the frosted pane greeting her return to us.

My father spoke to the back of my head when he said, "People lie to you because they don't respect you enough to tell you the truth."

I remained removed, brown eyes searching boundless skies.

"They'll cloak their words in omission, feigning innocence, thinking you're too foolish to recognize the lie." He paused, letting it etch.

I counted stars.

"That's what they're saying though. That they think you're stupid."

I yearned for Jupiter and Mars.

"The more deliberate and petty the lie, the less value they make of you."

I found Venus.

"You know you're utterly worthless when someone lies to you for sport." He reiterated and enunciated, "*Utterly.*"

I ran down the basement stairs to my bed that night, turtle-necking the covers, shivering myself to sleep. When my father jabbed me to say, "It's time to go get her," I was still tired and needing to stay put. But I dragged myself up, dressed and crept up to the living room to wait in the dark for him. I must have sat dozing there for thirty minutes before being bitten by the cold quiet. Automatous and groggy, I shuffled my way to the kitchen where I rubbed my eyes to read the numbers on the neon clock flickering over the sink. It was 2:38.

I stood still, listening as I looked harder and harder as if lodged in an illusion moments before reality dawns.

Climbing further up the stairs to the second floor, I halted briefly near my parent's bedroom door to sense my father sleeping-smug before I returned to my bed. There, lying dressed and fetal in my red rubber boots and matching wool earmuffs, I grasped the meaning of his fair-warning words. Oh, maybe not the exact definitions. But clearly the emotions. The shame of stupidity. The pain of worthlessness. The tears of contempt.

It's been 65 years, so I shouldn't still shudder, but, you know? Whenever someone chooses to lie to me — especially when it's one of those petty, deliberate, unnecessary little lies cloaked in omission and feigning innocence?

Sometimes, I still sob like a 7-year-old.

# # #

This refreshed essay copyright by Marguerite Quantaine © 2008 first appeared in The St.Petersburg Times.

## 19

CHARITY BEGINS ALONE

The vast majority of our mother's generation, and a large proportion of ours, behaved like perpetual damsels in distress by needing a man around to help them with the simplest things. They catered to the whims of every male entering a room, putting their needs first and foremost. They solicited men's opinions before making decisions, allotted them the larger share of food and drink, offered up the better chairs, turned over the greater control, and took whatever men claimed to know at face value in an endless effort to feed their egos. Above all, they needed to be married to a man and encourage other females within their inner circles to adopt the same medieval mindset.

Elizabeth's mom was like that. After Liz's dad suddenly died at age 72, she married four more times over the next 18 years.

My mom was just as assiduous in promoting women's

second-class citizenry *except* for getting hitched again. Nevertheless, being widowed at age 55 didn't stop her from relentlessly urging her daughters to marry and elevating the act of dragging men into every conversation and situation to an art form.

Once, after leaving a Broadway show at the Palace Theater in Manhattan, she grabbed the elbow of a man trying to maneuver the crowd outside the entrance, asking what bus she and I should take uptown.

"How the hell would I know?" he steamed at her. "Do I *look* like a bus driver for God's sake?"

"Well!" she huffed.

"That was Don Knotts, Mom."

"Where?"

"The man you just asked for directions."

"Andy Griffith's Don Knotts?"

"Yes."

"He certainly wasn't very polite!"

Okay, never mind that I'd been living in Manhattan for more than a year and had, single-handedly, succeeded in getting us to the theater from my upper west side apartment hours earlier after reminding her I knew the way because I'd been to the Palace Theater once before.

It was shortly after I'd won the Midwest Division of the National ABC Television Talent Hunt and was chosen to attend the American Academy of Dramatic Arts. I arrived in New York City on January 29, 1966, as a highly impressionable fledgling from a small Michigan town. My older brother Kit was in town on a stint working as a stagehand with the musical, *Hurray! It's A Glorious Day... and all that*, scheduled to open at the Theater Four on West 55th Street in March. The confidence he exuded pleased Mom, so they conspired long distance over the phone to persuade me to dress in my Sunday best and meet him outside the Palace at 9:30 that night.

I don't know why I was still trusting Mom's judgment of Kit. Not only was he chronically unreliable but as kids, he'd lure me into the scariest situations and leave me holding the bag under the worst of circumstances. We referred to these dupes as 'Kit tricks' — like when he dared me to ride a bike down dead man's hill in the cemetery without mentioning the bike had no brakes, or would lock me in the basement coal bin minutes before a delivery was to be made. Kit has always been my bad habit dying hard.

Regardless, since my 'best' was a blue silk bridesmaid dress worn to a July wedding five years earlier, I felt peculiar standing there with him fighting the dry cold wind, waiting under the marquee for the curtain to come down and the audience to emerge. Once it did, Kit ordered me to "just act natural" as we slipped under a velvet rope guiding a small procession of people invited backstage to greet the cast. Once inside the stage door, Kit abandoned me to look for Polly, a woman he claimed was a friend he'd made while working summer stock in New Hope, Pennsylvania.

The backstage of the Palace Theatre is cavernous with grips scurrying about in headsets, scenery on brails against brick back-walls, overhead catwalks several stories high and huge fresnel lanterns suspended from the ceiling. Alone and afraid of being caught, I stood in the center of the chamber looking like a lost soul seeking flight when the alley door burst open and down the long steel staircase came Kit's so-called friend, Polly, making her entrance while screaming, "Gwen, I'm here, Gwen, I'm here, I'm sorry I'm late, oh Gwen, I'm here, Gwen, I'm here!"

Upon reaching the backstage floor, she began barreling my direction until the redhead standing two feet away with her back to me pivoted on her black patent leather stilettos and asked, "Would you be a dear and hold my flowers so I can get a shot with Polly?"

As I accepted her large bouquet of scarlet roses, it finally dawned on me. I was backstage opening night of *Sweet Charity*, instantly cast as the unnamed flower girl in a publicity shot of the leading lady, Gwen Verdon, greeting her best friend, Polly Bergen.

Naturally, Kit was nowhere to be found, but something he'd said to me earlier proved my saving grace.

"No one will ask you who you are because they'll think you must be related to someone important — and not knowing someone important would be too embarrassing for them."

He was right. Nobody asked.

I waited until a bevy of friends gathered around the two celebrated stars before quietly handing the roses off and fading away.

When I got home, I called Mom and listened to her relate Kit's version of the evening—of how Polly was a no-show, so after I "ditched him" he joined a group of the theater grips and went downtown to the Red Lion to hang out.

I let it rest.

But whenever I revisit my very first night as a theater student enrolled in a New York City acting school, I can't help but think to myself, *Hooray! It was a glorious day. And all that.*

# # #

## 20

THE DOG DAYS OF DECEMBER

*T*here was this dog we loved and lost on Christmas morning, 1951. It changed everything.

Our home was a clapboard farmhouse built a hundred years earlier and insulated with Civil War era newspapers layered between the rafters and floorboards. Advertised as a White Elephant for three thousand dollars with nothing down, my folks bought the house because it was the only place they could afford. It was a rickety-rackety place that sweltered in the summer and shivered in the winter when no amount of coal heaved into the basement furnace could sufficiently heat the cast iron radiators or keep warm water in the boiler. The windows rasped with the wind, the floors creaked with the rain, and the back door often flew open unexpectedly.

"It's just a spirit visiting," Mom would say, having given up on getting my father to replace the antiquated latch.

We were born in that house, three brothers, two sisters and I. Our childhood was spent clamoring up and down its winding stairs, playing board games on its covered porch, wishing on the first seen stars in the night sky from its roof and never suspecting life would be any different than it was each day we were living it. We rode on broomstick horses and slid down grass-covered hills in corrugated boxes. We wore pillowcase capes and carried wood slat swords behind pie tin shields to battle imaginary knights. Summertime was spent camping at state parks in WWII army surplus tents where Mom boiled coffee and cooked meals over kindling fires while we faux-fished with pins tied to kite string and floated on boats resembling canoes of inner tubes wrapped in bleached jute twine. We scaled hills, charted streams, explored birch groves and scouted butterflies.

They were carefree years made all the better by the presence of a ninth member of our family adopted on the morning of my birth. Her name was Clancy. She was our family dog.

"It's written," claimed my mother, "that the original Irish setter wasn't the pure mahogany breed we see now, but a burnished red with a snow-white bib and matching diamond set in the center of its head." Our Clancy was born with both and — even though we boasted about the markings of her ancient pedigree — I secretly believed she was an earth angel.

Clancy was our comrade and confidante. She accompanied us on errands and whenever chores needed doing. She got us to school on time and waited there to greet us at the end of each day. She sat near the table when we ate. She stood near the tub when we bathed. She laid at our feet when we read. She watched over our well-being when we played. Games were intensified by her barking approval, birthdays were celebrated with her howling accompaniment, sorrows were soothed by the gentle touch of her cold nose on salt-streaked cheeks and many a bitter winter night was made warm by her body filling the cold void at the bottom of one of our beds.

But my *best* memory of Clancy is of Christmas morning in 1951 when we awoke to find her gone.

A fortnight before my father made his instructions clear. "Each of you is to make a list of everything you want for Christmas."

"Everything?" I asked, wide-eyed with surprise.

"What did I just *say?*"

I winced. My father was brusk at best and demanded obedience. That wasn't difficult since he worked eighty miles away and often forgot to check for compliance whenever he came home on alternate weekends. "*Everything,*" he reiterated, "no matter how ridiculous. Is that *clear?*" He stood glaring at our frozen forms before taking a Chesterfield from its crumpled cellophane covered pack, lighting it, removing a stray tobacco bit from the tip of his tongue and continuing on. "In one week, you'll each give me your list in an envelope with your name on it, and I'll mail them. Dismissed!"

My mom was as accommodating as my father was disparaging, encouraging us to always make amends after arguments and to always be willing to share our few possessions. "You six are the only people on earth you'll ever know your entire lifetime," she'd remind us. "Cherish that."

What began with cooperative glee quickly turned into the drudgery of pencil shavings, eraser residue, paper wads, and the sweet smell of spent crayons. Each night before bedtime we'd meet to exchange ideas, promising no duplicates would be recorded and agreeing that the first person to list an item would own it and regulate borrowing times.

"It's the perfect plan for maximizing returns," the boys assured.

"Who's Max?" I asked.

"Just do as you're told," they demanded, fully aware that I seldom did.

During our final review of lists, I learned that my brother Kit had added a P.S. to his list. "Dear Santa Claus," he wrote, "I want a puppy for all my own." Certain I was the only sibling who felt the same, I promptly drew a puppy on my list.

The next morning, our signed letters in sealed envelopes were handed over. As we stood at attention accepting a mutter from my father to "carry on," none of us knew that each of us had copied the request for a puppy originated by Kit.

Every Christmas Eve, Clancy rode with us on our journey to find a sweet smelling blue spruce, chop it down with a Boy Scout ax, tie it to the roof of our maroon Ford station wagon, and cart it home for trimming to the sound of carols playing on the car radio. The trips were always cold, cramped, and ripe for disagreement — but especially so that year when the predicted 'light flurries' became a heavy downfall. Even Clancy was agitated. She wailed with the whipping wind all the way home.

Mom slathered Big Top peanut butter on toast made from Holsum Bread for dunking in mugs of Ovaltine. Tree trimming required hanging aluminum-hinged Shiny Brite glass ornaments, thumb-thick multicolored Royalites, peppermint canes, silver tinsel, and a garland of popcorn and cranberries, all draped under a white plastic tree-top angel with spun glass hair and a die-cut skirt of yellow stars that glowed from one small bulb tucked inside.

The angel was near and dear to my mom. Each year she watched my father teeter on a chair to place it on the treetop, doing double duty as the signal for our time for bed. On the way upstairs, we'd stop at our red brick cardboard fireplace to thumbtack our stockings to its flimsy black mantel where Mom had balanced a glass of milk, sugar cookies, and carrots for Santa and his reindeer.

Even though Clancy scratched at our bedroom doors, her love wouldn't jump onto any of our beds to guard hearts that fateful night. We all ignored her pleas by forgetting her faithfulness, preferring the promise of a puppy.

A blizzard engulfed the house while we slept. The weight of its drifts barricaded the downstairs windows and forced open the back door.

Most mornings, the first boy up would check the fire in the furnace and shovel in more coal as needed. By the time he finished, the gas stove with its open oven door would be warming the kitchen and Momma would have oatmeal ready to quell our chant, "Food for the inner-man!"

But that Christmas morning was different.

We six awoke and sprang from our beds fueled by anticipation and oblivious to the unusual cold. We thread our way down the darkened stairs huddling close until Kit flipped the switch turning on the overhead globe illuminating a living room piled high with gifts. There were bikes and baseball mitts, sleds and skates, trumpets and teddy bears, dolls and drums, trains and planes, chemistry sets and butterfly nets, kites and cowboy hats, books and balls, clothes and caps lovingly wrapped and carefully arranged around our very first television set. It was as if all our wishes on first seen stars had been granted in one felt swoop and, thus possessed, we'd never again enjoy the luxury of wishful thinking.

Somehow, we sensed we'd committed the crime of excess by having everything we'd ever imagined as glorious within our reach. Yet instead of joy, we partook in a collective emptiness.

"Where's Clancy?" I wondered aloud, not noticing the absence of puppies. Twelve eyes darted in six directions.

"Here Clancy, here girl," Kit called out, whistling for her to come. We joined him in calling her. "Come, Clancy. Come!"

"She's gone," my father declared, already dressed to leave the house through a second-floor window, hoping to spot a sign of her from the porch's rooftop. "She got out the kitchen door last night and was caught in the blizzard. She couldn't get back."

"It's my fault," I blurted, my lips curled and quivering with regret. "I asked Santa for a puppy. That's why Clancy ran away. Oh, Momma," I blubbered, burying my face in her lap, "I didn't mean it."

Kit immediately confessed to asking for a puppy, too. And then, one-by-one, the others exposed what proved to be our family folly. Momma comforted us as best she could while watching the day die in our eyes. It was more hurt than she could bear.

"Kit," she urged, "check the bin to see if we have enough coal to last. It could be days before we get dug out of here, and there's no telling what's going on with the neighbors until your father returns. Take your sister along. Let her help you."

The steps to the cellar were thick-pitted pine, worn smooth on the edges from a century of use. I slid butt-to-step down them into the pitch black, whimpering, until seized by the sound of a soft, steady thumping.

"Is that the monster you said lives down here?" I whispered to Kit as he fumbled for the lights.

"I was just teasing about that," he hushed back. He grabbed my hand as the lone light from a hanging 25-watt bulb flickered on, shedding a soft glow directly below it. And there, in the corrugated remains of the television box was our tail-wagging Clancy proudly nursing *six newborn puppies*!

By the time the puppies were weaned, we'd assured my folks we were happy to share our one red setter. But it wasn't until the last of the litter was adopted that we realized we'd been promised and given everything we'd wanted for Christmas, yet none of us could recall what we'd gotten — except for those puppies we gave away.

Nine years later, Clancy died. We buried her in the back yard, her grave shaded by a pear tree my father had planted when she, the tree and I were all about the same size.

Thirty years would pass before the pang of joy replaced the pain of loss, and I adopted another Irish setter. She looked a lot like Clancy. She had the same white diamond on her head and crisp white vest on her chest. She was as loyal, as loving, and as totally trusting of me as Clancy was. I cherished her in every way.

But somehow, every year, there'd be those poignant moments when she'd remind me of a Christmas tree adorned in worn ornaments and popcorn streamers, a cardboard fireplace with Orlon socks dangling, a hard plastic angel, three little boys, three little girls, and the immense joy of modest presents to appreciate.

The holidays are and will always be a beautiful time of year. A time to remember that giving is its own reward, sharing is the truest joy, and love is the greatest gift.

A time and a spirit likened to, but never quite the same as it was — as *we* were — those long-gone dogs days of December.

# # #

This refreshed essay by Marguerite Quantaine © 1976 first appeared in The Antiquarian Magazine and as a limited edition, post card size, color illustrated and bound booklet circa 1995. As to be expected, the six siblings and Mom each recalled this particular Christmas with sparring memories over the years, but all agreed on the essence of it and the six puppy outcome.

INTIMACY MATTERS, LADIES

recent article in *Cosmopolitan* claimed 23% of twosomes are in couples' therapy.

These 'couples' aren't married or even engaged. They're simply dating and paying for therapy to see if continuing to date is an answer to the 'possibility' of spending a long life together.

Such might be simply a straight person fad, but I've detected serious flaws in dating requirement lists proudly posted on same-sex group sites, too, giving me cause to inter-pret the *Cosmos* figures as representative of how the concept of intimacy has changed dramatically over the past fifty years. It's now portrayed as less monogamous, more autonomous, shorter-lived, entered carelessly, exited quickly, void of regret, without expectations, and often treated like a group sport — as if the past cannot come back to haunt, and the need for instant gratification reigns supreme — right up until one person falls irredeemably in love with another demanding reciprocation.

Only *then* might flippant, insipid, trite, temporary, vapid, footloose and fancy-free implode in favor of discovering how intimacy shared between just two people committed to one another is elevated by recognizing the state of being *in love* as a blessing.

It's why falling in love feels destined.

If you truly want to grow old with the one person you love most, intimacy must be sacrosanct, neither trampled on by others nor diluted through the disclosing of what makes you as two, one.

Intimacy is more than being on the same wavelength. It's revealed in how attentive you become when your devoted consort enters the room. It's how close you stand and sit. It's there in the tenderness of talk and an eagerness to listen. It's brushing up against each other, repeatedly, in the course of a day. It's braided between glances, facial expressions, hand signals, terms of endearment, notes passed, cards inscribed, music played, words whispered, initials added to wet cement, carved in wood, and formed by toes in sand. It's in hands held while falling asleep.

Intimacy is also incognito as brooches, beads, bangles, bracelets, and bands etched in silver or gold and crowned with jewels accompanied by promises made. And as we age (especially those of us who are women loving women without heirs), we begin to wonder what's to become of our intimate tangibles?

No, not so much the house, car, or investments requiring named beneficiaries early on — but the special gifts, the private collections, the photographs, the love letters, the anniversary and birthday cards, the journals, the trinkets, the lockbox keepsakes. Who's to dispose of those? And what's to become of our rings?

These decisions, too, are intimacy matters, emblematic of what two women in love cherished about each other.

Historically speaking, older gay men have shown the tendency to become involved with much younger ones, paving the way to name their last dalliance as a beneficiary and leaving single men in their thirties and forties financially better off than they'd be otherwise. It's one reason given to account for gay men averaging the highest rate of disposable income in the nation.

Successful lesbians rarely adopt such pecuniary practices late in life. Instead, we tend to make the nieces and nephews we never knew (of siblings we seldom see) our beneficiaries. It might account for lesbians averaging the *lowest* rate of disposable income in the world.

I'd like to see us change that (sans the May-December male tradition) by women 'in the life' taking an interest in the welfare of younger lesbians who are making an earnest effort in their struggle to get ahead.

My hope is that more of our seniors will find and friend women who are 10-15-20-25 years younger; women who share our individual interests and personal values; women who demonstrate the kind of work ethic that proves a credit to our communities. Mentor them, fund them, gift them with something worthy of being treasured, recorded, and passed on to the future generations of 'us.'

The time spent needn't be intense, nor the gift substantial. It simply requires being significant enough to remind both the giver and receiver that people, like objects personifying their love, should never be taken lightly, nor disposed of easily.

No therapy required.

# # #

## 22

DRESS REHEARSAL

a week after my father died in 1969, my mom bought her burial dress, a long-sleeved bevy of beige chiffon accordion pleats with contoured organdy hemlines and cuffs resembling parched petunias.

The collar was fashioned into a multilayered sash cresting the shoulders and flowing down the back to veil the neck and screen the zipper. A peach taffeta sheath shimmered underneath.

"Everyone knows a wife dies seven years after her husband," Mom declared.

"Is that the law?" I asked.

"It is," she assured.

"And if you don't die, what then? Do they give you a ticket?"

Mom flashed me the look of admonishment that every parent keeps ready to actuate in times of insolence.

"It's a *glorious* dress," she said.

"Yes," I conceded. "A veritable work of art."

My mom was never as thin as she thought she was or planned to be. After 56 years, six children, and a passion for chocolate, she arrived at widowhood 20 pounds heavier than ideal for her 5-foot frame.

Still, she was striking. Her ivory-streaked ebony curls were invariably fastened atop her head like crown jewels. Her posture was precise. Her apparel was meticulous, with a penchant for pastels, fabric flowers, and contemporary styles.

The exception being that dress. Where other designs died on the rack and emerged in time as retro vogue, her burial dress remained permanently detained in 1969.

I don't know why Mom never saw fit to keep the dress in a garment bag. Perhaps she just preferred the convenience of instant viewing. Regardless, she carted it, unprotected, through five dress sizes, three homes, and thirty-seven more years.

"She makes me put it on, you know," my sister, Sue, disclosed one day.

"The burial dress?"

"Uh-huh."

"Whatever for?"

"So she can imagine how she'll look in her coffin."

I guffawed.

"She's serious," Sue cautioned. "Every visit, she makes me put that dress on and lie down. Eyes closed. Hands folded. Perfectly still. She makes Kate do it, too. Every holiday. But

Kate lies with arms stretched wide, like wings." (Kate's our kid sister. Both she and Sue are 5-feet-6-ish to my 5-foot-1.)

"Wings?"

"Yeah. When the sleeve pleats open, they look like angel wings."

"Why hasn't she asked *me* to try it on?" I almost pouted.

"Because you resemble a younger, thinner her," Sue teased. "She characterizes you as her little dolly."

I scoffed at her remark but took it as true. "So? How do you look in it?"

"Puh-lease," she chortled.

Maybe I spurned the dress because Mom acted ageless by never appearing seriously sick. Sure, her gallbladder dealt her a fit before she gave up donuts and she wrestled seasonal colds. But her heart was strong. Her wit was quick. She was ever valiant and resourceful.

Nevertheless, I phoned her every day after my dad died, until gradually what began as a daughter's concern for her mother's well-being turned us into cronies.

As we aged, I called more frequently. Mine was the first voice she heard most mornings and the last each night. In between, we'd chat over coffee, prepare meals via speakers, trade views of the news, and laugh at English comedies before retiring. An entire day's dialogue was condensed into less time than it takes most people to commute.

It was a fracture to her left leg that finally forced Mom to forfeit her independence for the security of Sue's care in San Antonio. Plans for us to move to Texas to be near her were delayed so she could visit Florida once again.

"I'll be there on my birthday whether you like it or not," she vowed.

"Only twenty-one more days until then." I grinned into the phone. "Are you feeling festive yet?"

"Actually," she said, "the strangest thing is happening right now. I'm watching my brain leave my head."

"What do you mean, Mom?"

"I'm not sure," she said softly. "It's so *odd*. I don't know where it's going or why. It just is."

"Like you're floating outside yourself, looking in?"

"No. I'm here. It's my brain I'm seeing go."

"Mom," I said. "You know I love you very much, don't you?"

"I... know... you... do," she echoed.

It was more of a blessing than a goodbye, those final four words of her life.

Three weeks later, on the morning of what should have been Mom's 93rd birthday, a package arrived from Texas.

While we'd been engaged in a dance of denial that she'd ever die, Mom added "cremation in my birthday suit" as a kind of codicil to her requests. Afterward, she painstakingly wrapped and lovingly labeled one last gift to me.

The dust of thirty-seven years has darkened the chiffon, but each pleat remains crisp. The organdy binding still echoes the contours of petunias. The taffeta slip still shimmers like skin. The sleeves, now raised, still mirror angel wings.

I encased the dress in glass and placed it as a watchtower over my desk where it's treasured as a testament to my mom, who always was what this dress truly is.

Glorious.

# # #

This updated essay copyright by Marguerite Quantaine © 2006 first appeared in St. Petersburg Times.

## 23

NEVER SAY NEVER — HOWEVER

I've never wanted to be rich or famous and can honestly say I've satisfied my wildest dreams in that department. It's not that I've lacked success, rather, I've lacked the desire to turn my success into a brand, popularity contest, following, or franchise whenever opportunity knocked.

That attitude stands at odds with the never-say-never person I perceive myself to be, especially since I know a slew of things I've never done. To wit:

I've never ridden on a roller coaster that wasn't wooden — however, I only rode a wooden one once, the Coney Island Cyclone in 1971. I still shiver from the mere memory.

I've never smoked a cigarette, or joint — however, I did spend my youth in New York City during the flower power years where I inhaled lots and lots of second-hand smoke.

I've never had a one-night stand — however, that's something one can always do (but can never undo).

I've never driven a car over 65 mph — however, I have been hit by one speeding faster than that.

I've never won nor lost an award for anything I've authored — however, I know if I'm ever willing to pay the application fee required to get nominated for an award, I might, at least, lose.

I've never grown a tomato plant that bore fruit costing me less than $5 per worm infested tomato — however, I'd gladly pay $5 for a tomato that tasted like the beefsteaks eaten off the vine back in the day.

I've never run a marathon — however, I did once win the fifty-yard dash in 7th grade, marking the last time I ran anywhere, for anything, ever again. (Also, I discovered I have flat feet.)

I've never chewed tobacco — however, I have crammed enough packs of Bazooka bubble gum into my jaw at one time to make it look like a wad of Skoal.

I've never cheated on an exam — however, I don't play cribbage without a crib note.

I've never tried Spam — however, I was warned I'd flunk Spanish if I didn't stop speaking it with a French accent, so I transferred from Spanish to French class only to be told I spoke French with a *Spam*-ish accent.

I've never dissected a frog nor mounted a butterfly — however, I did accept a 'D' in 8th-grade science rather than do either (way back before it was against school board law to opt out).

I've never donned a little black dress — however, I do own a little black dress I'll never wear.

I've never worked at a job I didn't love — however, I have quit every job I've ever loved in due time.

I've never had my heart broken — however, I've often wondered if I've ever broken one.

I've never eaten oysters — however, I have been (OY!) slimed.

I've never acted like a call girl — however, I did assist a Broadway actress starring in a role as one.

I've never stayed for the length of a Major League baseball game — however, I did get hit in the head by a Detroit Tigers fly ball in the third inning of the only game I ever attended.

I've never learned how to swim — however, I did (at age 65) float for the first time after inserting ear plugs.

I've never eaten organic candy that could compare to a Clark bar or a Snickers — however, I've contemplated doing so. *Not!*

I've never spent much time with anyone from Canada — however, I have spent way too much time with Canadian Club.

I've never tasted a praline I didn't devour — however, I'm always up for the challenge.

I've never been to Paris — however, I did once duck for cover when the Concorde came in for a landing over our heads while we were stuck in traffic on the expressway near La Guardia Airport.

I've never left food on my plate at a dinner party — however, I have pilfered and disposed of many a dinner napkin filled with food that wasn't appetizing.

I've never encountered a stray dog or cat I didn't rescue if it would let me — however, I have broken every promise I ever made *not* to rescue another stray *ever* again if please, pretty-pretty please we can keep just this one last one.

I've never ridden a horse up a mountain trail — however, I was thrown from a horse down a hill.

I've never been an extra in a movie — however, I have starred in a nationally syndicated television commercial.

I've never seen a shuttle launch — however, I did risk being arrested when I slipped under the rope to sit in a space capsule at the Kennedy Space Center.

I've never simply said 'yes' upon being asked by a waitress if I'd like a cup of coffee at the end of a meal — however, I do always say, "Only if you've just now made a fresh pot, otherwise, no."

And I've never made myself a bucket list — however, this could probably pass as one.

\# \# \#

## 24

SEEING RED

*M*y mom hated to have her hair touched. It prompted her to enroll in beauty school for the sole purpose of learning the best way to style and care for her own thick, black, naturally curly locks. I still have the leather bound 1935 textbook from her beauty school days that she abandoned upon deciding to coil her hair and pin it atop her head like a crown of glory. It was very attractive, even enviable, and she never fashioned her hair differently from then on until the day she died seventy years later.

I suppose that's why it came as no surprise in the summer of 1958, when I was still eleven with shades of natural auburn and blonde streaking throughout my wispy thin, straight as straw, mostly mousey brown hair that Mom suggested I choose one of the three colors and dye it.

I chose auburn. Clairol's Sparkling Sherry to be exact. It perfectly matched my auburn undertones and duplicated the color my older sister, Sue, had chosen to dye her hair a year earlier. It cost 85¢ for a glass bottle of the dye and another 25¢ for a bottle of peroxide. You mixed them together in a plastic squeeze bottle before applying and waited 45 minutes before washing the gooey residue out with Halo shampoo and rinsing with diluted Heinz red cider vinegar.

"The dye coats each strand. It doubles the thickness of your hair," Mom promised.

"Do I still use vinegar?" I questioned her even though I already knew it helped to untangle wet hair and kept it glossy.

"It prevents the color from looking unnatural."

That fall, I began the seventh grade as a redhead the same as Sue had the year before me. Whenever anyone asked us why our brother Michael had black hair, we'd confess, "He dyes his."

The new school was larger with thousands of students. None of the students I knew in elementary were in my classes, nor friends of mine in junior high. Consequently, everyone I met from then and since have only known me as a redhead.

Including me. Because changing your hair color enhances your personality. And even though Clairol has updated the names of their colors, I've remained true to those streaks of natural auburn chosen as a child.

I've never sought to discover the adult dominant-color of my hair. Through junior and senior high and college, a stint as a kosher camp drama counselor, New York City careers, a Florida business and wherever else I traveled or settled on living, once every month I've found a place to be alone for an hour for the solitary purpose of denial in dyeing.

I'm 72 now. I've never let my hair grow out, but if I did, it would be an all-over silveresque, the same as it is at my temples that I leave untouched so the age of my face won't drastically contrast my crown that sports a hairstyle I haven't changed in decades.

I am my mother's daughter.

25

IMMORTAL KISS

$\mathcal{E}$ighty days after Bobby Kennedy kissed me, he was killed. I'll never fully understand why it happened — either the kiss or the killing. Each time he was caught up in the joy of the moment. Both times he got whisked away.

As happenstance had it, Kennedy was frolicking with friends in the back seat of an inconspicuous car crawling down Fifth Avenue when he spotted me — a young, vibrant, redheaded Breck replica in a Kelly green, worsted wool coat, weaving through revelers lining Fifth Avenue for the St. Patrick's Day parade.

I was pugnacious. The flock in front of the 666 building was so sardined, it turned my two-minute sprint to the Prime-burger into a twenty-minute tussle. Hearing the crowds crescendo as a car of paraders slowed to a stop behind me, I poised myself to push through an advancing pocket of people.

Suddenly, someone grabbed my elbow and pivoted me into his arms, gently tilting my chin upwards before planting a quick kiss. His thicket of hair reflected like flax in the midday sun veiling two hazel, sleep stripped eyes conferring a dilatory blink — not unlike that of a tomcat purring thanks. Then, just as instantaneously, he was hustled back to his locus in that long procession trekking toward his untoward future.

"You're never going to guess what happened to me," I nudged my friend Marion during the elevator ride up to our offices at Fuller & Smith & Ross the next morning. "Bobby Kennedy kissed me."

"Ohmigod, ya gotta be kidding!" Marion gasped. "What'd'ya do?"

"Do? What could I do? I was stunned, that's all."

"Did anyone see?"

"Well, yes. I guess. How could they not?"

"I mean, anyone *here*. Because it might not set well. Him being in the running now and all."

That hadn't occurred to me. "It was just a kiss," I dismissed.

"Yeah," Marion nodded. "But Bobby *Kennedy* for cripes sake. Who gets kissed by a Kennedy?"

"Who doesn't?" I scoffed.

Fuller & Smith & Ross is an advertising agency footnoted in history. As Manager of Purchasing & In-House Printing, I'd been privy to a confidential meeting detailing departmental procedures for handling the 21 million dollar account we'd secured two months earlier. My first assignment was to have business cards engraved for our new client. The inscription: Richard Nixon, 577 Chestnut Ridge Road, Wood Cliff Lake, New Jersey 07675.

Upon completion and delivery to his Park Avenue address, Nixon graciously sent me an autographed card. Seeing his inked signature on that ivory colored Bristol board proved pretty heady stuff to me, a small-town transplant and political novitiate. I was young, eager and altruistic; a cookie-cutter copy of that last generation of Americans who hadn't a true clue as to what went on inside our nation's governing bodies or outside our autonomous lives.

So, while I excelled at my job of vetting vendors, overseeing offset runs, getting offices decorated, equipment updated, carpets cleaned, forms designed, prototypes printed, supplies stocked and locks on doors changed whenever a colleague left, it wasn't until I was entrusted with the billing of telephone lines linked to a network of chameleon operatives that I started to sink with the sinking-in.

"Cause and effect, people," was the daily drill. "Never has so much money been amassed to elect a candidate. Our targeted buyouts of principal advertising airtime will efficaciously shut the Democrats out. Cause and effect."

Try to remember or imagine: In 1968, PBS was still in the proposal stage, there were just three major networks, prime time was essentially over by 10 p.m., a 30-second spot in the top-rated markets cost about ten grand, and a million dollars was an unimaginable sum to most. But 21 million? That was *whew*!

By day, Nixon commandeered town hall meetings answering random questions in primary states while being filmed at three angles — front, back, and side. By night, our media technicians removed audio from side and back-shot tapes, replacing it with Nixon voiceovers of perfected responses. These were the videos utilized by the media for viewing and airing. This was the foundation for creating many of the 15, 30, 45 and 60-second spots and news feeds. Apparently, audience participants were so elated at seeing themselves on television that they failed to notice Nixon's edited answers. At least, I heard no rumors of suspicion outside the office. I saw no evidence of complaint. But within our ranks, long hours involving similar scenarios and the disillusionment such capers caused was taking its toll.

Perhaps that's why Kennedy's assassination registered as an amplified aghast to us. Because by the time he announced his candidacy, we'd already been entrenched in a predetermined campaign victory for ten weeks. I was given reason to believe everyone working on the inside of both political parties knew this from the get-go. Our jobs seemed only a matter of proper execution.

Sure, Bobby Kennedy added glamour and excitement to the illusion being painted for an impressionable public. Sensational headlines and endless editorials promised he could change things. And would.

But factuality was, by the time Kennedy won the California primary, every projection we'd been made privy to in January had confirmed itself by June. Ad copy, speeches, rebuttals, and press releases were written and delivered verbatim, leading a nation of primary voters to the polls and persuading them to push the Republican button. We knew if the Democrats had been wealthier in '68, only the names would have changed as a chimera to protect the process.

It's no wonder a spate of shame beset our rank and file the day Bobby Kennedy was assassinated. His was an incomprehensible loss for no comprehendible reason. Arguments erupted. A mutiny ravaged the art department. Secretiveness ensued. Most of us continued to carry on until the battle was won in November... but long before then... we were lost.

So it's little wonder I and others resigned after Nixon's victory without revealing the true reason for our departures, i.e., that suffocating feeling of complicity and defenselessness when slapped in the face with reality, relentlessly.

As a souvenir I kept the screen-printed Peanuts prototype of Snoopy endorsing the Nixon/Agnew ticket that was spurned as a possible campaign poster by our California office after Charles Schultz objected. Saving it from the art department garbage seemed somehow fitting. I put Nixon's business card in my pocket. I surrendered my two tickets to an Inaugural Ball. I left my 18kt gold RN lapel pin in an ashtray on the desk. I signed the purchase order to change the locks on my office door.

Marion and I were alone on an elevator going down when she asked, "Did you ever think of yours as his kiss of death?"

Angst kept me from answering.

"You know," she nudged. "Cause and effect. It's all we've heard for eleven months."

"So?"

"Well, go figure. If he hadn't stopped to kiss you, he'd have been five minutes faster for the rest of his life. He'd have finished his speech and left the hotel, alive. Maybe you were put on earth to slow him down. So he could meet his destiny on time. D'ya think?"

"Gee, Mare. Thanks for that," I groaned. "And, no. I *don't* think."

But, yes, I have.

And yes, I do, occasionally, while maneuvering crowds. Crossing streets. Riding elevators. Hearing cars slow. On one March morning and one June afternoon. Whenever wearing Kelly green.

And ever since.

\# \# \#

This refreshed essay copyright by Marguerite Quantaine first appeared in The Antiquarian Magazine © 1985, More © 1995, Venus Magazine © 2011 and margueritequantaine.com © 2013.

THE QUALITY OF JOYFUL LONGEVITY

*W*hile individuals of a certain age are asked for their secret to longevity, couples remaining together for decades are often urged to reveal their recipe for happiness. And even though most invitations are staged before cameras producing edited soundbites, the one thing partici-pants agree on out of earshot of the press is that only the *quality* of time is essential.

Upon learning that 60% of society is younger than age 50, we speculated we've been in love longer than the majority of Americans have been alive.

No matter. The fact remains that the quality of joyful longevity depends on a continuous curve following life as the lesson of the day and — like history — whatever isn't learned is doomed to be repeated with someone else.

Here are 49 things we've learned in 49 years of being in love.

1. Sound sleep requires laughter lastly.
2. Recognize early that the favored parent is emulated, eventually.
3. Lose at fault-finding.
4. Compliment a meal before adding salt.
5. Whatever is collected will someday be hoarded.
6. Think romantically.
7. Please and thank you are BFFs.
8. Holding hands while arguing is a hearing aid.
9. Listen with your entire body, inside and out.
10. Fight rhymes with flight.
11. Neither caress less nor roar more.
12. A simple touch is apology enough.
13. Lower expectations except of self.
14. Have music playing in at least one room whenever home.
15. Speak softly and turn a deaf ear.
16. Think kindly about things remembered.
17. Don't keep score.
18. Never hurt intentionally.
19. Tears have deeper meanings.
20. Leave sentimental notes in unexpected places.
21. Be both the best of you and the best of others.
22. Always ask what is needed, first.
23. Giving what you want is taking.
24. Offer your own opinion last, or not at all.
25. Pets make us better people than people can ever hope to be.
26. A single child will never share as readily as one raised with siblings.
27. Serve coffee with a kiss.

28. It's not life, it's living. It's not death, it's dying. It's not fear, it's fearing.

29. Levity is imperative.

30. Two televisions are better than one remote.

31. Be of mirrored ethics.

32. One comfortable bed in a home is enough.

33. A cloth table covering, cloth napkins, and a fresh flower, nightly.

34. Gush gratitude.

35. Make here the better place to be.

36. Slow dance under every full moon.

37. Send a card by snail mail a minimum of monthly.

38. Keep a joint journal.

39. Sleep in the buff.

40. Insolence provokes anger.

41. It's neither the lie nor the cover-up. It's the enabling.

42. Say what you mean the first time.

43. If in doubt, don't.

44. A know-it-all never is.

45. Keep a path cleared down the middle of the room.

46. Love is sacred. Belittling it is blasphemy.

47. Yes and no questions need one-word answers.

48. Biting your tongue hurts less than what you shouldn't have said.

49. The odds of the person loving you most being the one you love most is *not* 1-in-a-million.

It's 1-in-7.3 billion.

# # #

AS GOOD AS GAY GETS

*S*omeday my novel, *Imogene's Eloise*, will be optioned by a mainstream publisher, rate stellar reviews, be adapted to film reflecting its eloquent romantic innuendo and receive the acclaim of people who'll prattle over my sudden success.

Sudden? The math dare's to differ.

The fact is I've worked hard all my life to get to be as old as I am, where I am, with whom and how we got here.

I began my adventures at age 5 by collecting castoff bottles for return to wooden crates at the corner, single pump gas station with its big red Coca-Cola cooler of soda immersed in ice water and a grease monkey teetering on a beat-up stool next to it paying me a penny a find.

At 7, being small and scrawny for my age, my brother dressed me as a waif and sent me out to knock on the doors of upper-class condos, poised to sell the occupants Christmas cards they probably never sent, but gave me my dollar a box because I looked so pitifully poor (like a melancholic mutt on the street corner wagging its tail, twanging their untuned heartstrings).

At 8, I shoveled snow with a spade in the winter (that's right, a spade), pushed lawnmowers in the summer, and raked leaves in the fall, underpaid with nickels by anyone willing to exploit me.

At 10, I delivered newspapers on my brother's routes. It required me to rise before daybreak, cut the hairy nylon jute twine from big bundles left on a nearby street corner, roll and fold each paper to perfection before burnishing and stuffing them into a canvas bag that I dragged along behind me, pitching the papers toward subscriber's porches, then hurrying home in time to don a dress and walk a mile to school.

At 14, I claimed I was 15 to get a genuine job (4-9 week-days, 9-9 on Saturday) selling records at a store that only hired boys for the 30 years before I sailed through the door.

"Why should I hire you?" asked the owner, a doddering Dickens-like character whose bifocals were as thick as block glass and modish flattop belied his desire to appear younger. "Boys bring in girls who like records."

"Boys flirt with girls that giggle and irk paying customers," I countered. "Boys arrive late, leave early, take cigarette breaks and call in sick from phone booths at football games." I let that set a second before adding, "I'm a redhead. My skin is flawless without makeup. I'm cute enough to attract boys who'll talk to me about girls. I'll sell them records for those girls. Whenever they win one over — and they *will* with my expert advice — they'll be back to buy more."

"Expert advice?"

"I have three drool-over older brothers and one tall, bomb-shell of a sister. I've heard all their game plays. I know exactly what to say to seal the deal. Try me. You'll see."

He did, teaching me purchasing, cataloging, product display, inventory control, advertising, and promotion. I was the first girl ever hired there, then the first girl hired as the historical research editor for a locally based trade magazine, then the first girl hired as a proof-runner for the daily news-paper before I finally fled my hometown for the big city beat.

I arrived in New York with $126 lining my red rubber boots, no job prospects, no place to live, and no plans beyond attending the American Academy of Dramatic Arts where I'd earned an entry after winning the regional finals of a televi-sion talent search in which I'd been unknowingly entered. Being awed and alone in Manhattan was thrilling. Every direc-tion I looked felt like an arrow angled upward.

All I had going for me on my first day of faking it was the attitude of, "Oh sure, I can do that." It gained me the gig of being the first female hired as a graphic artist on the in-house magazine at the United Parcel Service even though I'd never seen a T-square, held a razor knife, or knew how to crop a photograph. After several months of intense covert tutelage by the fellow at an adjacent artboard, I snagged an enviable job in the corporate offices of an international Fifth Avenue adver-tising agency where I was promoted in five months to be the first female Purchasing Agent inducted into the Purchasing Managers Association of New York. Within three years, I parlayed that into a corporate office fashion industry junior executive slot where I excelled until being struck by a drunk-driven taxicab.

The driver flew the coop, and the cab company declared bankruptcy, as did the insurance company holding the cab's policy. It catapulted my career back to ground zero accompanied by chronic disabilities.

But by then, I'd fallen in love, so instead of being solo and stalwart, I was half of a daemon duo with four even starrier eyes. Together, we built our own Long Island ad agency and launched three magazines while moonlighting as registered gumshoes.

So let me offer all you younger bootsies with advanced degrees and greater expectations some humble advice chiseled out by glass-ceiling crackers from the boomer years: Stop dwelling on fame, fortune, and acquiring the entrapments that rich-quick dreaming brings. Focus, instead, on loving the process of living and the person you're living it with. If you do, you'll succeed at whatever you choose, even by making a living as a writer, or an artist (the two puniest paid professions on earth).

No, I've never won an award, and my name is unrecognizable to all but a few blog followers, fogeyish editors, and finicky clients. But I'm still in love after 49 years, and along the way our diligence bought 11 vehicles (6 of them new) and paid off 3 mortgages, ultimately nesting us in a 1931 vintage home, debt free, with time to complete my first novel at age 66.6.

And even if the movie version of *Imogene's Eloise* gets released posthumously — *so what?*

All I ever truly dreamed of as a child was for the chance to find one great love, the talent to write one great book, and anonymity on the streets.

Life really doesn't get any better than that.

I kid you not.

# # #

A CAUSE FOR CELEBRATION, 1972

*T*he preliminary police report rendered me dead upon impact.

A drunk driving a Marathon cab fitted with an extended, reinforced steel bumper had broadsided us. He was clocking up to 70 in a 30-mph zone when he ran a red light and collided with our VW Bug that I was easing into a parking spot as Liz sat next to me in the suicide seat.

The impact was ferocious. While peripheral vision allowed me a glimpse of my killer, there was no other warning. No screeching of brakes. No screaming of pedestrians. No sense of impending doom. Just a mild feeling of astonishment before whispering, "Oh my God, I'm dead."

Our car was ripped apart (lengthwise) from hood to trunk, welding the sheared pieces to the front end of the taxi. Our flung wreckage had come to a halt twenty feet away at the entrance of a branch bank. I hung down twisted and broken through the remains, my face hovering just above the pavement, my auburn curls resembling a red rag mop.

Most gay couples are drawn and quartered by such tragedy. They're impeded by laws awarding jurisdiction to distant family members. They're intimidated by protocol and prodded by propriety. Their feelings and wishes are summarily dismissed as irrelevant. Barred from the ambulance. Excluded from intensive care. Denied decision-making.

"She's my sister," Liz lied, emphatically. It instantly ended any question of her authority.

The first time she lied was to the officers who barricaded the wreckage, then tried to restrain her from reaching back for me. They'd dragged her clear, insisting I was beyond help.

How she broke loose and what transpired is a wonder.

I responded to the energy of her touch. I warmed to the blending of her tears in my stone-cold eyes. I sensed the silent incantations of her heart imploring mine to hold the course of 'us' as one against all obstacles and odds.

"Hey, babe!" I breathed.

Her second lie was to the ambulance attendants. The third, to emergency room doctors. The fourth, to nurses. And then to technicians, aides, and investigators. She didn't hesitate to claim me as her sister, knowing involuntary deceit had long been coerced from gays in lieu of being banished and public humiliation. Lies were once our only conceivable lifeline. In many communities across America and the world, they still are.

Fortunately, I was a corporate executive for a large conglomerate. It gave me special insurance privileges that provided her with unlimited hospital access. She stayed in my room. She partook in every detail of my care and was privy to all my medical information. My doctors consulted her. My nurses kept her updated.

Nevertheless, when it came to certain courses of action, not everything suggested was automatically allowed.

It's because, even now, most lesbians mistrust the medical profession. We cringe at the prospect of contact with male doctors. We shy of probes pertaining to our personal lives and intimate behavior. And even though many older women entered conventional relationships in an effort to hide their true sexual inclinations, there are vast numbers of lesbians who have never engaged in intimacy with a man. Women who know being a homosexual goes far beyond an aversion to heterosexual sex; that the differences in our genetic codes include wiring that circuits a deep-seated aversion and basic incompatibility with all dominant aspects of the opposite gender.

Liken to the scientific distinction between Asian and African elephants being designated as a different species because they'd never *voluntarily* copulate, homosexual females and homosexual males will never *voluntarily* copulate with the opposite gender. Just as heterosexuals instinctively react to homosexuality as aberrant behavior, homosexuals instinctively react to heterosexuality as aberrant.

So it came as no surprise to Liz when I refused to be catheterized by attending doctors even though catheterization was necessary to save me. Regardless of the brutal total body trauma and fractures suffered, this perfectly natural anomaly triggered my sense of aversion and challenged my dignity, demanding decorum. Only the empathy and courage of the emergency room surgical nurse, Christine M. Tekverk, could clear the emergency room of males and provide me with the symbiosis I needed to survive.

Nearly forty-seven years have passed since the crash that forever altered our lives.

I insist the change was for the best even though I pass each day in fluctuating degrees of pain. I still walk with a cane and sleep with my neck and left leg braced. My brain still spasms (albeit on rare occasions), jerking my head violently to the left. My hand sometimes trembles and body sometimes buckles. My ears still burn shades of crimson whenever my emotions run high or my energy runs low. I still suffer from PTSD.

And although I can never sit for longer than 30 minutes at a stretch, nor walk for longer than five minutes without resting, nor stand on cement surfaces for *any* length of time — from all outward appearances you'd never suspect there was anything amiss with me.

No criminal proceeding ever materialized since, back then, drunk driving was a misdemeanor. And it took well over a year before the civil action found its way onto a court docket. By then the driver had vanished, while both the taxicab company and its insurance agency filed for bankruptcy. That left New York State to assume jurisdiction over the proceedings. I was told it would only approve payment of a dime on every dollar litigated with a preset ceiling attached.

My lawyer said to settle for $30,000 against bills that would total more than ten times that over the years.

"Why?" I asked.

"Because you lied about being sisters," he said. "If we go to court, that lie will come up. It's a character issue. You'll have no presumed credibility."

"A *character* issue?" charged Liz. "Whose character?"

My attorney remained silent except for his shuffling of documents.

"The drunk driver?" she asked. "His employer? The insurance broker? The court demanding a decision?"

"Settle," he suggested a second time.

"And if I don't?" I challenged.

"I'm not certain my firm can work a trial date into our calendar. I'm afraid if you don't settle, you'll need to find other representation."

So I settled. Because, honestly? I was just so happy to be alive, grateful for every second of every extra day.

"And when you think about it," Liz reasoned as we left the courthouse heading home, "for the rest of our lives they have to be them. But we get to be us."

It was a cause for celebration.

# # #

This refreshed essay copyrighted by Marguerite Quantaine © 2002 first appeared in the 3rd person in The St. Petersburg Times, in the 1st person in Venus Magazine © 2010, and referenced in the novel, Imogene's Eloise by Marguerite Quantaine © 2014. My unwillingness to risk the safety of my partner, my pets, and myself demanded I cloud my identity as a precautionary measure.

HAPPY DANCE OCCURRENCES

I never leave my fingerprints on any surface other than pants and shirts, not necessarily my own. Call it obsessive compulsive disorder (because that's what I'm told it is), expediency is key to me cleaning my hands. If something foreign gets on one, anyone standing near me can expect a spontaneous pat on the back.

A compulsion to keep my hands clean has been with me since grade school where I refused to finger-paint without a brush. Chaos erupted when, after seeing me get my wish, *all* the kids wanted one. It dubbed 'fastidious' as my signature modus operandi.

Newsprint became my professional nemesis. As an art and antiques columnist for a string of east coast trade papers during the late '70s and early '80s, I was commissioned to do an article on 19th century Commonplace Books. These over-size tomes were maintained by women in lieu of journals, decorated with pressed flowers, studio and vista cards, idioms, autographs, photographs, news clippings, and exquisite chro-molithographed die-cuts of animals, birds, bouquets, angels, hands, hearts, and holiday images — no doubt the forerunner to modern-day scrapbooking.

In hope of gaining a personal perspective, I tried keeping a Commonplace Book — and failed miserably. I claimed it was because I feared damaging the vintage die-cuts I'd collected. But truth be told? Elmer's Rubber Cement did me in. After several frustrating attempts, an editor suggested I settle for substituting the text of one daily commonplace occurrence of joy instead. I never completed the actual assignment, but I am still keeping the book.

These are some randomly selected commonplace occur-rences recorded over the years.

May 9, 1976

Elizabeth's mother doesn't drink alcohol. She says it makes her elbows weak.

February 20, 1983

Mom recounted her search to update her wardrobe today. "I saw a dress where the tag was marked seven hundred dollars, and I said to Jesus — did you *see* that?"

April 20, 1985

On the way home from Hartford after midnight, tonight, it was pitch black and overcast, and we were lost. I insisted we stop at a closed down, boarded up gas station on a tiny triangle of land in the middle of a forked road so I could locate the North Star, which, as it turned out, I couldn't find it if it was sitting on my nose. But wouldn't you know, there I was, standing atop our VW Bus — bothering *no one* by the way! — when a cop car pulls up, lights flashing, sirens screaming, and an officer gets out.

"Just what are you doing on top of your van at this time of night, miss?"

"I'm looking for the North Star so I can find the direction to the highway that gets me back to New York before sunrise," I justified.

He calmly pointed the beam of his flashlight to a huge green-and-white sign indicating we were five feet from the US 1 South New York entrance.

March 30, 1991

Working as a team, we simultaneously set off all the talking and musical stuffed toys on display at Walgreens tonight. A manager came running.

September 22, 1996

It's Sunday and still pouring sheets of rain. When we went to pick up the papers, I spotted a poor old dog lying hurt in the gutter at the edge of the Methodist church parking lot.

It enraged me! The mere *thought* that, even though the parking lot was packed with worshiper's cars, there wasn't an indication anyone had stopped to help that poor dog. I loudly denounced the depraved indifference of people in general (and this group in particular) as I jumped out into the deluge, only to discover the dog was both dead and drown to boot.

I make no apologies for the blubbering that overcame me as I dialed 911. They promised to send an officer immediately. In the interim, we dashed the four blocks home and back to get a clean, dry burial blanket to wrap the dog in. We returned just in time to flag the animal control truck pulling up.

After conversing briefly with the officer — a kind and sympathetic man who recognized, even through the blinding rain, how distraught I was — I gave him the blanket before I kneeled down into wastewater and petted the mongrel, apologizing for the cruelty of mankind, and blessing its soul and spirit, asking that I might always strive to be the best of it.

Between sobbing and the downpour, I was pretty much waterlogged, making it a struggle to get up before motioning to the officer that it was time. As he leaned over to drape the blanket, the mutt jumped up and ran away.

June 19, 2000

Before heading back to Michigan today, my mom hung a pair of her underwear on the pink room's doorknob to dry, along with specific instructions. "Leave them there because I have plenty of panties at home, and I'll know right where to find them on my next visit."

December 22, 2003

Elizabeth spent an hour tonight making me a gift by

putting three pieces of rounded wood together with staples, tape, string, nails, and no logic whatsoever. To her finished 'triangle tree' she wound some gold yarn, spacing it here and there in an attempt to create goddess-only-knows-what. It was touching to watch her engaged in an earnest endeavor.

Tiny tributes to the endurance of love are cemented within stolen moments such as these.

Today

Okay, I guess there's no sense in my trying to deny it. These tidbits have my fingerprints all over them.

# # #

30

MISS EDNA'S HEARTIFACTS

I never danced on a grave, but I did steal something from the dead once. I spied it, stood on a stool, pried the four corners of it loose, flattened it against the belly beneath my blouse and walked away without contrition.

It happened one sultry late-summer day when ocher leaves are as omnipresent as the sun a half-hour before high noon. I felt myself liquefying in line while waiting my turn to take a number.

"Who was she?" I asked the fidgeter in front of me.

"Nobody," he said.

"Everyone is somebody," I suggested.

"Name was Miss Edna," drawled the clerk recording the details off my driver's license. "You be biddin' on the house?"

"I'm sorry?"

"Cuz it hasta be moved. Otherwise, it'll be bulldozed in two weeks' time. Land ain't fer sale. Yer number seventy-six. Next!"

. . .

The house was one of those classic Cracker shacks built on a farm axed out of a forest that encroachment slaughters and sacrifices to almighty developers. Where highways supplant front yards claimed by eminent domain.

Miss Edna's epitomized such woe, its slats of ill-fitted wood slapdashed together before being embalmed in asbestos shingles that, over time, the sun had blistered into coarse curls. Rust stained the ridged metal roof, inside and out. You could peer through her windows and peek through her walls.

"Did you know Miss Edna?" came a voice.

I turned to see a wisp of a girl, all blond and bowlegged in mismatched plaids and stripes with dangling plastic beads being balanced on broken fingernails.

"No, I didn't. Did you?"

"Of her, mostly," she conceded, evading my eyes as she spoke in halting speech as broken as her spirit. "Mom died birthing her. Dad made her pay for it till he croaked."

"Never married?" I asked.

She sighed. "Eloped on horseback to the (Ocala National) Forest. Honeymooned camped down by the Silver River. But the old man hunted them with dogs. Beat the boy bloody. Strapped his broken body to a horse and jest whipped it on away."

"Dead?"

"So's been said. Dragged her back and got a judge to — you know — wipe all records?"

"Expunge."

"Expunge," she nodded. "After that, he treated her like

scum. Least is, that's how I heard it." Sniffling, she turned away and ambled off. "A kind woman. Always kind."

The contents of Miss Edna's home were displayed without a modicum of dignity. Dozens of handmade patchwork quilts had been unceremoniously dumped on makeshift tables. The balance of her belongings were heaved from windows, shoved off porches, or dragged by the brown paper bag full into the red clay yard and left to decay until sold to the highest bidder. Some were busily rifling through the offerings, looking slyly around for watchful eyes before switching contents from one numbered boxed-lot to another, intent on stealing a better buy.

Feeling vicariously forsaken, I found myself standing alone in Miss Edna's pillaged kitchen. The fusty stone fireplace yielded remnants of charred chair legs, rags and rubbish sprawled onto gnawed linoleum exposing holes in sagging floorboards. A rubber hose running through an outside wall was tied to a wire clothes hanger nailed to an overhead beam and aimed at a gray metal washtub. It was flanked by a contaminated toilet and corroded sink, all exposed in shamefaced view of anyone entering unexpectedly.

The rest of the house was bone bare, except for an unsung satin dress bequeathed to the back of a closet door, a laundry tag dating from 1931 still pinned to its mother-of-pearl buttons.

And there, thumbtacked to the wainscoting above the lintel, hung a small, red, cardboard carnival sideshow sign with bits of silver glitter flecking off an embossed exalted face and two words.

"Jesus wept."

\# \# \#

This freshly edited essay copyright by Marguerite Quantaine © 2010 first appeared in The St.Petersburg Times.

31

BEING MERYL

*I*magine you are Meryl Streep sitting in the audience, nominated for a Best Actress Oscar at the Academy Awards and Golden Globes, and Mia Farrow's name is called instead of yours.

It doesn't matter that a vast majority of the general public and international acting community think — make that *know* — Meryl Streep is the finest actress to grace a screen since the talkies. And it doesn't matter that her performance far outshines that of any other actress on the planet. She must sit and smile and be grateful to know that she's the superior actress, even when saddled with being lesser so by those who are neither as talented, nor as accomplished as she.

The point is, being the best at what you do is never enough to win the acclaim of those around you. Rather, the chances are it will elicit exactly the opposite results regardless of your profession. Because that's the nature of awards and winning and — *especially* for the craft of writing — book reviews.

I emphasize *especially* because book reviews and letters to the editor are two of the three outlets within the media where everyone, regardless of their intent, intelligence, honesty, or lack thereof can participate as an authority. The third is the installation of a five-star system that can also prove to be the weapon-of-choice for malcontents.

As a result, the question we all must ask ourselves is: Am I complicit?

The answer is YES if you:

(1) Write a good review for your friend or relative simply because she *is* your friend or relative, not because her/his book is as good as the review you've given.

(2) Award a five-star rating to a book because it was authored by a friend or relative, not because her/his book is as good as you've rated it.

(3) Issue a bad review for a book you haven't read.

(4) Issue a bad review for a book you haven't read because you carry a grudge against the author or you have a friend who carries a grudge.

(5) Award a low star rating for a book you haven't read.

(6) Award a low star rating for a book you haven't read because you carry a grudge against the author or you have a friend who carries a grudge.

(7) Sabotage an author whose publisher is in competition with your publisher.

(8) Sabotage an author for revenge.

(9) Sabotage an author out of jealousy.

(10) Sabotage an author because you *can,* and that ability gives you power.

If you're an author, you're wondering how this essay became about you instead of that so-in-so who gave you a bad review.

That's the thing.

When it comes to writing — just as when it comes to all other areas of life — it's never about what is done to you. Rather, it's always about what you did to help create an atmosphere where such injustices flourish. And by 'you' I mean 'me' and 'us' and 'we.'

Like every other journey, this one takes one step by one person at a time. It takes resolve. It takes a decision by each of us to (1) refrain from giving credit where credit isn't due and, (2) refrain from sabotaging those we don't like and, (3) choose to learn from those whom we consider to be more talented, more creative, or more accomplished and, (4) mentor all who are receptive in an effort to improve our craft and writing community.

It isn't necessary to like every writer. But we must try to respect every person who makes the effort, takes the time, and risks the rejection that results from writing a book regardless of its caliber.

And if we can do that, we will know our own worth.

And if we can do that, we will rejoice in the success of others.

And if we can do that, we will accept, as a burden, that there will always be those whose low self-esteem, jealousy, envy, ego, or anger won't allow them any other recourse but to lash out.

And if we can do that, we'll realize the next essay, article, story, or book we write will be better because of it as a blessing.

And if we can do that, we will each — we will *all* know — what it's like to be Meryl Streep.

# # #

THE TELLTALE HEART

*P*ublicly, Thomas Jefferson believed in the principles of freedom. But privately, Jefferson grappled over whether the worst white man was still better than the best black man.

Ultimately, Jefferson's failure to champion equality left his own illegitimate child enslaved, opening the wound which has since defined — not the competency of his mind — but the capacity of his heart.

Until June 25, 2015, justice still floundered at a crossroads governing the use of fine print to qualify equality. It was then the Jeffersonian paradox challenged whether we as a nation believed the worst heterosexual was still better than the best homosexual. Because all the *worst* heterosexuals could marry throughout America. But even the *best* homosexuals could not.

As the Supreme Court stripped away the righteous rhetoric and political posturing, it's possible they recognized a raw reality, i.e., even when heterosexuals committed the most heinous crimes (murder, rape, child molestation, spousal abuse, terrorism, treason, and crimes against humanity), their known deviant behaviors were ignored by American marriage laws.

However, even when homosexuals proved model citizens, their single alleged aberrant activity was predisposed. The court must have then questioned whether that spoke to the heart of who we truly were regardless of what we professed ourselves to be.

On the one hand, we insisted the purpose of marriage was a belief in the sanctity of family.

On the other hand, we ignored the fact that millions of felons sitting in high-security prisons were predominately heterosexuals possessing marginal moral character at best. Yet each had a right to marry.

In some sat the suspects and convicts held for complicity in the 9/11 and Boston Marathon attacks, all of whom retained their legal right to marry in every state.

But Lily Tomlin did not.

Charles Manson, Sirhan Sirhan, David Berkowitz, the Menendez brothers, Theodore Kaczynski, James Eagan Holmes, and Dzhokhar Tsarnaev could.

But Ellen DeGeneres could not.

The former slaughterous dictators Saddam Hussein, Osama Bin Ladin, and even Adolf Hitler, could have.

But Kate Smith, the American icon of our anthem, *God Bless America*, could not.

If the Court entertained the position that "sin" be the foundation on which law be defined, would it validate the proponent "hate the sin, not the sinner" premise? Could it then ignore evidence that it wasn't "sin" being shunned, profiled, attacked, ridiculed, denied equal rights and murdered? Only American citizens were.

Would the Court ask why no marches were being planned, political wars waged, or state constitutional amendments against the seven deadly sins? Would it demand to know why it was only a singular Bible reference declared as an abomination being targeted? And if it determined the sin/sinner assertion was simply an inflamed edict, could it set precedence for other inflamed edicts as just-cause to alter constitutional law?

If the Court had recognized the Ten Commandments governing the worship of other Gods, building graven images, working on the Sabbath, blasphemy, dishonoring parents, murder, adultery, stealing, coveting, and bearing false witness as written-in-stone — would it be compelled to admit that being gay was not?

Politicians and pundits insisted same-sex marriage was un-American, implying we could no longer sing or live up to the words in *America the Beautiful* if we allowed marriage to be maligned. They contended — like that esteemed song — the institution of marriage has been declared our national heritage and pride.

But only the Supreme Court could decide which American citizens qualified as entitled to inalienable rights, and which (regardless of their American birthright and exemplary character) did not.

Until then, the justices were forced to reflect on one of America's finest homosexuals, Katherine Lee Bates, who felt, authored, and gifted our nation with those cherished words,

"And crown thy good with brotherhood, from sea to shining sea," while in love with another woman for 25 years.

History had the Supreme Court in a chokehold.

On June 26, 2015, America forever changed when the Supreme Court decided it was time we stopped cherishing a broken institution that denied equality to our totality and, in so ruling, bound us by law to cherish each other *instead*, by making marriage equality the law of the land.

# # #

This freshly refreshed essay copyright by Marguerite Quantaine © 2004 was first published to benefit L.I. Pride.

## 33

IN DREAMS I WALK

Sometimes life is a sleepwalk in which we see everything clearly and deny it. My walk began when I was fourteen, five weeks before the Fourth of July in 1961. I had a recurring dream.

It was dark and raining. I saw myself asleep on my grandma's couch. Something stirred me. I got up and walked to the kitchen. There, lying curled up on the floor was my grandma — my Mom's mom. I knelt down and reached for her hand. Only then would I realize my eyes were open and staring at the ceiling.

Every night for five weeks the same dream.

The morning after the first time, I told my sister Sue. She said I was being dramatic. The second time, I told my brother Kit, who told my mother I was being weird. After that, I went on dreaming the dream but never spoke of it again.

On July 2nd, the weather forecasters warned of rain for the extended holiday weekend but promised clear skies for fireworks by the Fourth. I had a job selling 45s at the only record store in town. By closing time that Friday, I knew they'd been right about the rain. My brother forgot to pick me up, forcing me to walk the half-mile home in a dismal drizzle.

I hoped my mom was working the vigil shift at a hospice home by then, unaware of my whereabouts. All I wanted was to crawl into bed and sleep through the holiday. And I might have. But Mom and Kit were in the living room arguing over my grandmother when I sneaked in.

"I wouldn't ask. But I *must* work," she was saying. Frantic and sorrow strained her voice. "Go? Just for tonight?"

"Nothing doing," dismissed Kit. "I've got plans for early morning. Besides, David's living with her. He's the one who should be there, not me."

"Your brother won't be there tonight, and she's not well," Mom pleaded. "She needs you." He ignored her. "*Please?*"

"I'll go," I said, disarming them. Without time for questions or concern, Mom gazed her gratitude, and Kit drove me to where I'd never go again.

It wasn't magnanimous of me. I idolized my grandma. Had circumstances demanded I live with her for good, I'd have gone as willingly. It's not that I didn't adore my mom. I did. But Mom said she loved the six of her children equally. Grams loved me *especially*.

My grandma was the scent of boiled coffee, fried donuts, and brown soap wrapped in the warmth of a summer day. A stern, determined woman who lived alone on a quiet street, in a plain house, without television or telephone. Though her isolation required Mom's visiting daily, she clung to her privacy and possessions as if they were gold. (They weren't — not even gold-tone.)

By eleven, the rain turned fierce with roaring thunder swallowing the sky. Kit dropped me and skirted, feeling no obligation to either escort me or check on her. I had to pound hard on her raised-paneled solid wood and frosted beveled glass door before Grandma heard me and let me in. She immediately demanded to know the whereabouts of my brothers.

"They couldn't come," I lied. "I came instead."

"I don't want you," she said. "I want Kit. Where's David? I want David."

She sounded slurred, as if the storm had scrambled her senses.

"Well, you got me, Grams," I said. "So let's get you to bed. I'll sleep in the living room on the couch."

It took some fussing before she shuffled back to the bedroom. I sat with her in the dark a while, making certain she was settled before gently kissing her cheek good night. Then I returned to the couch and lie down damp, intent on sleeping fast.

When a silent streak of lightning crept by the window, I realized my eyes were open. There was no thunder. No rain. No noise. Only that bright white transient light marking the moment and where I was.

I rose as if by habit. I headed toward the kitchen, coming to an abrupt halt at the sight of a radium dial clock on the countertop. The hands read ten past three.

Looking down, I saw the outline of my grandma curled and lying on the floor. I knelt. I reached. I took her hand. Remaining there. Motionless. Frozen to the touch.

Slowly, I stood, backing my way to the couch. I lay down and feigned sleep. I opened my eyes, focusing on the ceiling. Then I got up and retraced my steps. Approach, kneel, touch, return, sleep, refocus.

I did this over, and over, and over, and over, until the clock's face was fixed at six. The sun was filtering through the window, bathing her by then. I knelt one final time before walking to the bedroom to check her bed. Finding it empty, I searched for life of her in dresser drawers.

Eventually, I returned to the kitchen carrying a pillow to comfort her head and a sheet to warm her. Three separate shades of white.

And there I sat until I heard the doorknob rattle and the zest of my mother's voice calling "Momma! Momma!"

Death wakes us up in ways that never let us sleep so sweetly again.

# # #

This refreshed essay copyrighted by Marguerite Quantaine © 2003 first appeared in The St.Petersburg Times.

## 34

HUSH, HUSH, SWEET CHARLATAN

*M*y sister Kate believed in truth. She thought she recognized it, practiced it, and that it would always prevail.

But I'm not sure truth ever was or can be. Nor am I certain of its prevalence in society today since all alleged truth stems from whatever was written *before* us, as if verified as absolute fact. And given that even the most inspired of wordsmiths are writers-at-soul, we each must choose from multiple abstracts of speech, edicts, merged thoughts, external influence, doubt in some entities, unbalanced confidence in others, and a necessity for meticulous punctuation in order to advance beliefs — all while knowing the end result will be subjected to individual interpretation using multiple mediums regardless of the author's intent.

Enter the innate willingness for many to automatically believe whatever is being told them and — worse yet —

parroting those narratives as if each utterance was an original thought from which errors can be justified by citing a misdirected faith in the charisma of charlatans dressed in fleece.

Please don't get me wrong by taking me out of context.

I harbor no objection to faith. It's an effective, convenient, efficient, popular, time-honored tradition that's both easier to embrace than most of us are willing to admit and necessary for the survival of both the fittest and unfit.

What I question is an inclination to believe the worst in others, as if in doing so we'll esteem ourselves to those whose alliance we crave.

What I find dubious is our rallying to deny rights to those unwilling to join school cliques, group cliques, office cliques, organization cliques, political cliques, and awards cliques.

What I cannot fathom is the instant exclusion of those we've never met nor ever spoken to based solely on what's been heard from a friend, relative, or associate about a stranger.

Think of how many times you've united against bullying in our schools over the past decade, assailing the abusiveness of name-callers as detriments to society.

And yet, sixty million Americans voted for a name-caller to lead this nation and participated in the notion of locking up a person who has never been indicted, arrested, booked, tried, or convicted of any crime in her lifetime while another hundred million Americans capable of taking action chose to do nothing at all.

In a patriarchal society (which ours is) I can understand how misogyny can flourish among males. But the implausibility of misogyny is such that I cannot understand how it thrives among females!

Except... I do?

Perhaps it's because every news anchor, commentator, journalist, politician, and figurehead over the years fail to question the ecclesiastical elephant in the room.

I first recognized the enormity of its presence forty-two years ago when I refused to attend my brother Michael's wedding.

At the time, I'd been in love with my Elizabeth for seven years, a woman who'd not only been crucial to saving my life after a catastrophic car crash, but had eagerly, earnestly, and single-handedly tended to my long-term recovery for five of those seven years. Nevertheless, the invitation to my brother's nuptials didn't list Elizabeth's name, nor did it include her as a plus-one option.

As a result, I declined the invitation.

Now before you feel any indignation on my behalf, please, *don't*. Remember, it was 1977. Homosexuality had only recently been declassified as a mental disease, while me and mine remained labeled by law as felons at risk of being sentenced as such. We were outlaws, social misfits, deviants, and, worse yet, a cause for embarrassment.

Even now, there are communities in America where being homosexual is portrayed as justification to detain, although not prosecutable; municipalities where dissident gender profiling can divert police from responding to assaults, or delay ambulances from arriving in a timely manner; where medical treatment is subpar and getting away with causing a death as a result could go unnoticed or be ignored altogether. (It's at this you should take umbrage.)

My brother's wedding was viewed as a big deal because, of six children (all of us then in our 30s), only two were married. It was likely his union would mark the last chance for my mom to be a mother-of-the-intended ever again. So, even though it was discreetly discussed and agreed that my Elizabeth should have been invited, I was nonetheless demonized for my decision not to go — right up until the portion of the actual ceremony where the bride agreed to *obey* her husband. It caused my sisters and mother to storm through our front door several hours later echoing each other.

"Thank *God* you weren't at the wedding, thank you, thank you, thank you, thank you, oh my God, *thank* you for not coming! You would have caused an uproar. Even we nearly did!"

It's true. They knew me well. I've never taken kindly to being submissive to, or even particularly respectful of, male authority. At very least, any sacred pledge to obey would have made me gasp conspicuously, if not trigger an audible spontaneous, "No-o-o!"

Which returns us to those questions unwritten by journalists, unspoken by news anchors and commentators, unsought by pollsters, unaccounted for in election booths, unstatesmanlike in Congress, unaddressed by constituencies, unadulterated, unanticipated, unalterable, unapologetic, unassuaged, unappeasable, unsettlingly, unstudied, and (perhaps) unassailable, untouchable, untenable, and even unrighteous in the final analysis.

But not un-askable.

Does a woman's pledge to obey her husband require being dutiful to his choice of candidates when she is casting her ballot?

And if so, does that mean America has become a Silent Theocracy?

# # #

A LOVE NOTE IN PASSING

*F*rom the moment she was born, everything was wrong and everything was right about Buzzbee.

Her mother, YokoOhNo, was a Corgi chained to a stump in a neighbor's backyard, left out in all kinds of weather, inclement and otherwise.

On the sly, we freed Yoko of incarceration each weekday while the owners were at work from seven until seven so she could accompany us in walks around the neighborhood and romps with our Schnauzer mix, Oliver, a one-time forager for Yoko that the neighbors chased out of garbage cans. Oliver led us to Yoko after we rescued him.

But on the night of January 11, 2000, the lights were bright in the neighbor's house and the family was home, ignoring the howls of Yoko trembling in the bitter cold, pleading for mercy.

It seemed only natural that we crept through the cover of darkness to steal her, breaking the chain around her neck and ushering her to freedom. We made her a bed in our garage out of an old folded, king size, goose down comforter arranged on a three-tier egg crate mattress placed near a 1500-watt forced heat, oscillating heater. Before retiring, we promised her we'd keep her at any cost. We left her food, water, dog biscuits, access to the outside dog run attached to the house and a friendly feral cat to keep her company.

The next morning, we found Yoko had somehow managed to quietly give birth to eight puppies.

Three of the pups hadn't survived, but of the five that did, we found a home for one — Ethel — once she turned nine weeks. Afterward, we cried our eyes dry and swollen for two days before deciding to keep the remaining four: Alice, Chin-Chin, Buzzbee, and Sparky.

Only Buzz was riddled with benign tumors the size of golf balls bulging out of her coat, tags hanging from every leg, perpetually leaking-crusty eyes that eventually went blind, and allergies to all forms of commercial canine food, leaving her bald from the middle of her back to the tip of her tail. Her heart and ears were too big, her lungs and paws were too small, and the vet wrote her off as most likely to die before her first birthday.

But Buzz displayed an inherent ability to adapt, an abundance of love, infinite devotion, and spunk. While the other puppies thrived, she endured all that plagued her with grace. She was happy, attentive, loyal, and ever grateful. She never whined or cried and only barked when a stranger walked by the house. She never growled. She never disobeyed. Even as a puppy, she never made a mistake in the house.

Counting Oliver, Yoko, Tinkerbell (our Pekingese), and Blue 2 (our Golden Retriever), we'd grown to an eight dog household overnight that fated evening. But by 2015, all but Buzz had passed away — until we lost her on May Day, peacefully in her sleep at 15 years, 3 months, and 19 days.

Each tear shed for the numerous dogs and cats that have enriched our lives is laced with immeasurable gratitude. They've all been fine friends of gentle courage, providing us with purpose, guidance, and genuine joy.

"Bless their souls and their spirits and may we always be the best of them."

# # #

EVERY WOMAN SHOULD RUN

FOR PUBLIC OFFICE

"There's never been a colored, a Jew, a Democrat, a Yankee, a queer, or a woman as mayor of this town and there never will be!"

I glanced up from my notes to study the odd little man in his Oshkosh overalls, Penny's plaid shirt, knee-high Frye boots, and Tom Mix hat. His cohorts called him Red. I don't know if he was christened that or nicknamed for the color of his neck, but it certainly didn't stem from shame felt or embarrassment by him or any of the men at that district Republican Committee meeting rewarding him with whistles and a rousing applause as I sat alone in the far back corner of the small auditorium, taking notes on the forum as a favor to the absent president of our local Republican Women's Club.

Yet all I could think was — what luck!

I wasn't a committee member so I couldn't object without risking the security of self. But I was born in the small town that hosted the first Republican convention in Jackson,

Michigan, under the oaks on July 6, 1854. An obscure granite rock with a bruised bronze plague once sat on a tiny patch of treeless grass three short blocks from where I spent my most misinformative years.

A hundred years later, in the same town, the rites of passage included adopting both the religion and political party affiliation of your parents. My parents were protestant and Republican. I'm neither, but during my juvenescence, I pretended to be both.

The reality is, religion and politics have never been roadmaps nor roadblocks for me. I tend to accept that we're all going to believe what we need to believe in order to survive our slippery slope slide from here into the hereafter. However, the *pretense* of politics alarms me, and it's the reason I always encourage women to run for public office.

I have.

It's easier than you think and more satisfying than you dare to imagine.

After filling out the simple forms with the Americanized spelling of my last name, and paying a nominal filing fee, I learned you aren't required to raise money, put up signs, hand out cards, take out ads, stand on street corners in inclement weather inhaling exhaust while waving to commuters — or even to serve if elected. All of which I did not do.

Instead, I entered the citywide race for mayor because I *could*. And because I learned the mayor was in charge of the police force that allegedly created computer software profiling every resident according to age, gender, race, religion, political affiliation, marital status, and *coded lifestyle*.

I ran because the mayor had the power to veto city council legislation. I ran because the personal voting records of all residents, their addresses, and phone numbers can be made available to campaign camps via their candidate. I ran because it's possible for local elected officials to access sensitive census information about their neighbors.

Ultimately, I ran to be given equal time to speak at all candidate gatherings, lunches, forums, debates, and media interviews, followed by unlimited time to answer questions. Places where I could tell the people about the profiling, veto capability, records reality, and potential for both discrimination and profiteering to the detriment of the electorate should the information be misused by unscrupulous officials with a personal agenda to advance.

But chiefly, I ran because I was told by a Party head, "You cannot."

"And yet," I said, "I can."

"You can't run as a Republican."

"Unless I'm registered as a Republican. Then I can."

"It's a nonpartisan race, so no one will know."

"Unless it's leaked."

"You won't have the backing of the Republican Party."

Aye, and there's the sub rosa.

Most of us like to think we're supporting a candidate who shares our convictions and has our best interests in mind.

Go. Run for any public office. You'll quickly learn it's the Republican National Committee (RNC), the Democratic National Committee (DNC), and the corporations funding them that dictate the conversation, feed the media, and virtually run this nation by Charlie-McCarthy-meets-Jerry-Mahoney tactics, where those connected contingents channel all the money solicited from donors into the war chests of the candidates they've pre-selected to win.

Furthermore, the nominees of both the RNC and DNC sign a Party platform pledge to toe the Party line in order to receive the financial clout of the RNC or DNC, because the chances of winning an election for those who don't sign — *even on a local level* — are zero, zip, nada, none, and nil.

Oh, and get this! Those war chests can be used to funnel funds for phone banks to robocall citizens matching their frequency and their voting history at the polls on odd, even, and no-show years. They can funnel funds for surveys with contrived questions for the ostensible purpose of suggesting nonexistent improprieties practiced by the opposing party. They can funnel funds for spamming newspapers with testimonial templates to praise one candidate, or deride the other, or push an agenda, or create confusion, or imply majority support, with each letter signed and sent by a party faithful — so it *appears* to the public as an original thought and legitimate concern rather than a parroted message. They can funnel funds for business owners to be visited by party members offering recommendations on which candidates to support, along with the insinuation of how less profitable it would be to lose a customer base of political party members. They can funnel funds for whisper campaigns leaked to small presses controlled by deep pocket party-pleasers linked to online sites willing to post disinformation.

The strategies for beating your opponent are all outlined

(or were when I ran) in an instruction manual detailing how to sway an election to a preferred candidate with news stories clouded by opinion. Where the media inserts the suggestive words 'could, might, alleged, contend, claim, may, and if' in place of the absolute words of 'can, is, are, and will' to report a 'possible' truth. Where newspaper corrections to falsehoods are buried in places seldom noticed or read. Where editorials aren't required to be factual.

But this ancient paraphrased maxim still rings true: *The most dangerous woman in the world is the one who can't be bought.* That's where running for political office serves as the American dream. Because running to lose by having the gall to tell the unmitigated truth assures your voice being heard.

And isn't that what we all want? To be heard?

When I ran for office, my words were so well heard, by the time election day rolled around, they'd been stolen and used to further the campaigns of others running for even higher offices. A willingness to freely let your words and ideas be claimed by others is how you help change happen. Not by sitting behind a safe screen typing out rhetoric about what's wrong with the country and who's to blame. And not by writing a check, convinced your donation will contribute to making this nation better and stronger.

Instead, *run for office.*

Attend every avenue available for you to stand up and speak. Recognize freedom of speech for the priceless gift it is. Say what's in your heart. Ignore naysayers. Concentrate on connecting with real people and experience the exhilaration that comes from putting your mouth where your mind is.

In the final analysis, the financial reports (required to be filed by all candidates) indicated the incumbent spent an average of one hundred and twenty-five dollars per ballot cast in his favor, while I didn't spend a dime.

On election night, I lost by less than 75 votes. Not once. *Twice.* Because the following year, I ran for school board and lost by another narrow margin.

Whew!

\# \# \#

## 37

THE IMPORTANCE OF BEING ENCOURAGED

*M*Y MOTHER ENCOURAGED me to become an actress because it's what she first wanted to be. She encouraged me to marry and have children because she wanted more babies. She encouraged me to be an artist because I worked as a specialist in black-and-white 19th century illustration adaptation application, and she delighted in coloring my artwork.

But she never encouraged me to be a writer. Even though I was steadily employed as an editor, columnist, and essayist for periodicals most of my professional life, I rarely ventured beyond being an editor and freelancer until after my mother passed away in 2006. Only then did I begin writing my first novel, *Imogene's Eloise*.

Seeking, needing, and wanting approval from unwilling parents might be the first obstacle every child endures. It quiets confidence.

But if you're possessed by the desire, or are willing to

perfect the skill, or are blessed with the talent, you'll eventually begin to find an audience of strangers and delight in any kernel of encouragement.

It's been rumored that Amazon, with its multi-millions of titles, doesn't begin pushing the sales of a book until 50 reviews have been posted by verified buyers.

I don't know if that grumble is true or not.

But let's suppose it is. Fifty confirmed reviews is a lot to ask of readers and expect for any book, especially when most of us abide by the standard "if you can't say something nice, say nothing at all" rule of etiquette. The primary flaw in such protocol occurs when an author knows, or even suspects, you might be reading her book. By censoring yourself out of kindness you inadvertently, (1) contribute to author-angst and, (2) prevent a genre you enjoy from being recognized by the mainstream media.

Trust me when I say, if LGBT genre books are ever to secure safe haven in society and attain the respect all well-written ones deserve without sacrificing the virtues inherent to our culture, we need the attention and support of the mainstream media. And we need it — not just for the token spotlight of gay celebrities who can afford armed guard public protection, or live in walled private estates, or travel within a select circle of friends mirroring themselves — but for the community that joins in exalting those privileged few while being baffled by continued anti-sentiment toward homosexuals.

Could it be that acclaimed lesbians and gays are elevated as the untouchable ideal while the uncelebrated community is ignobly real? And if so, isn't it time we cease living in their illusory shadows by working to better define our own?

Before he died in 1882, the English author, Anthony Trollope, insisted a novelist must, through a framework of personal ethics, inspire readers to identify with a book's characters and, in so doing, act in a manner that benefits humankind.

I might have failed in doing that.

While vigorously welcoming and greatly appreciating enthusiasm shown for our efforts, I'm fearful of the reviewer who settles on simply saying, "It's entertaining."

Yes, novels need to please, first and foremost. We should neither expect, nor hope for more.

And, yet. I do.

I hope for a reader who will ponder both the obvious and the subtext in my words and feel emboldened, or is healed of hurt, or resolves her past, or embraces her present, or is enlightened to the levity that life seeks as nourishment in order to survive well.

It's not that I won't appreciate whatever praise I receive or fail to feel gratitude regardless of my ranking in the book world.

And it's not that I don't know in my heart, if my mom were alive today, she'd forego the content of what I write in favor of coloring the book cover.

It's *all* encouraging.

\# \# \#

38

LAST RIGHTS

The last three words my sweetheart and I speak to each other before hanging up the phone are "I love you." We say the same in public places whenever going our separate ways, when exiting the house either alone or together, and before falling asleep each night. Often, I even say them when leaving her to tidy up the kitchen as I head upstairs to write. The words are always heartfelt. They're never flung. Never forgotten.

I learned to say "I love you" from my mom who believed we should say it to our siblings whenever one of us walked out the door. We didn't. The words were always a given between Mom and me and similarly exchanged between my kid sister Kate and I. Otherwise, I was reluctant to express them.

I don't recall my father ever saying the words to my sisters or me except as part of a tickle poem intended to torture us, especially Kate. He was a misogynist when it came to his daughters and superfluous to our unwanted births. Admittedly, I neither felt nor uttered the three word sentiment to him.

It's no secret that my father wanted six sons, having cast himself as too virile to spawn females, so I can't speak for my brother's relationships with him. Besides, the three boys were all older, coming of age when the practicing of sexism thrived. They've remained distantly connected to me for most of my life — not as antagonists, mind you. There's no ill will. To this day, our communications are always polite, respectful, and engaging. But we're more like casual friends with certain secrets kept than we are siblings with a shared past. Our family skeletal closets are firmly sealed.

To wit, I doubt they know, immediately after returning home from an involuntary 48 hour stay in the mental ward of Foote Memorial Hospital, tethered to a bed by brown leather straps with gray metal buckles and warned via a whisper to my ear, if I ever told anyone what happened I'd get more of the same — I tried to kill my father with a salad fork. Where I found a salad fork still baffles me. Salads were never part of any meal plan when we were children, save for the lettuce-less Waldorf variety, and even then, only when Michigan Macintoshes were plentiful.

Admittedly, patricide by salad fork seems tame by today's road rage standards, but in 1962 small-town Midwest America, even the hint of such news would knock the kid washing his duck in the kitchen sink off the front page (or at least lower it below the fold).

I was fifteen, five-foot-one, and tipping the scales at 75

pounds to his five-foot-eight at twice the weight. He quickly overcame me with a grip from behind, but I chomped down on his left hand until I reached the bone of his index finger. Tossed off and aside, I spit blood when warning him to never to raise a hand to Kate or me again. He never did. He and I steered clear of each other ever after.

I've never cried for my father nor regretted my actions, remaining reticent about the motive behind my foiled intent of fifty-seven years ago. I do not talk about the details even now.

And, really, what would be the point? My brothers, who saw no need and made no effort to protect their sisters from him in the past would only doubt us now. They have their own cemented memories of him. Whereas my older sister still grapples with hers.

But no one talks, unless you count my father, whose callous and cunning correspondence to my brothers bemoaned his life, made excuses for his failures, alluded to addictions, transferred infidelities, and emulated martyrdom while praising his sons before claiming his redemption. Letters that were copied and given to my sister Kate as — what? Proof of his greater goodness and professed regret?

She left me the copies with a not-so-cryptic note attached, written in her own hand, confident I'd understand how it felt to be lost in a world where forgiveness is now the fad and forgetting is always the fallacy.

No, no. It hasn't made me bitter. Just mindful. And weary.

Mom said my father was watching the Detroit Lions battle the Cleveland Browns on television when his eyeglasses fell off. While reaching down to retrieve them, he suffered a massive heart attack. Before the thud, she heard him curse.

My father's final words were, "God damn it!"

My mom's final words were, "I know you do."

Kate's final words were, "I love you."

# # #

## 39

LEST WE FORGET TO REMEMBER

*W*HEN I WAS five, we lived in a century old farmhouse. It had cast iron radiators to warm it in the winter, wafer thin linoleum covered floors, pull-string overhead lighting, and a narrow pine brown painted staircase just inside the front door vestibule with nine stark boards heading straight up before snaking left for three more and leveling off to a thirteenth step at the top.

Facing directly ahead was the bedroom I shared with my two sisters. At the end of a hall papered in remnant rolls of Depression era patterns was a bedroom for my three brothers. And flushed with the wall to the right was the entry to a closet containing a second, much smaller door inside leading to an exposed beams, unfinished attic without floorboards.

"Never, ever, under *any* circumstance open the door inside the closet at the top of the stairs," my mom forewarned us. "Because if you do, you'll fall through the ceiling. And then don't come running to me. I *told* you not to do it!"

Let's be clear. Mom always added the disclaimer of "don't come running" to her instructions so we'd know better than to get caught. But she never added the words "and die" to an edict. That would have implied definite danger. Ergo...I went ahead and opened the door.

It wasn't that I was a bad little girl or even an overtly rebellious one. I simply had a ferocious curiosity that challenged every easy, accepted, purported, and fabricated reason given to blindly follow orders.

And, anyhow, it was all *Alice's* fault — she being *Alice In Wonderland* from the animated Disney film Mom had taken us downtown to see at a Saturday matinee in 1951. Our subsequent incessant playing of the film's score from a set of eight, 78 RPM Little Golden six-inch records ensured I knew every word and melody, making it Alice who implanted the lyrics to Very Good Advice in my mind as a mantra, and Alice who told me to open the door and search for a lavender and white striped Cheshire cat in a garden of talking flowers.

Unlike Alice, I needed no key to unlock the door, nor was I required to eat a mushroom in order to shrink myself for passing through it. Even though the inner closet portal was considerably smaller than a standard door, I was still elfinesque at five and could easily slip through it.

I might have opened the door to a virtual sea of history if only I'd known how to read the century old newspapers crumpled in layers as insulation there. Since I couldn't, my focus zoomed in on the solitary object sitting in the slanted roof room — a flat top, slatted oak, seasoned pine steamer trunk wrapped in inch wide black lacquered tin ribbons, Moiré

Metalique corner plates, and latches on each side of the lollipop-looking lock hanging open.

My fearless feet were smaller than my age, allowing me to scurry along the beams like a ballerina on a tightrope. I reached the trunk with ease. Opening it proved somewhat of a struggle, but the anticipation of releasing a fat lavender striped cat far outweighed the weight of the lid. When I pushed it up, the top plopped backwards as I fell forward, landing on a black jacket with brass buttons the color of dirty mustard. Wiggling back out, I slowly tugged the jacket after me, dragging it to my side out the Alice door, through the hallway door, and into my bedroom.

The jacket was my found fortune from a treasure chest. I marveled at the buttons, their background bumpy to the touch, with a spread-winged bird standing atop a broken cross in its claws. I'd heard the word 'war' without knowing what war was. I could not conceive of what war did and wouldn't comprehend what a swastika signified for many years to come, so these beautiful buttons appeared more as coins to me. I'd found gold!

Certain my mom would feel as thrilled as I about my find, I put the jacket on, and, with the sleeves dangling down long over my hands and the bottom of the jacket threatening to trip me as I shuffled along, I scooted down the stairs, one step at a time, toddling through the dining room and into the kitchen where my mother stood washing breakfast dishes at the cast iron, wall-mount, white porcelain sink.

She stopped, turned toward me and stared as if stunned before asking, "Where did you get that?"

"Through Alice's door," I beamed. "Inna trunk!"

"Upstairs? In the attic?"

I nodded vigorously.

After a moment, she reached for my grandma's black-handled sewing scissors and approached me. Kneeling, she gently removed the jacket from my shoulders before sitting back on her bent legs and slippered feet, systematically cutting off each bird button. Upon finishing, she checked the pockets and found a folded scarlet band with the broken black cross imprinted inside a white ball. She scissors-shredded that, too, before doing something she'd also told us never *ever* under any circumstances to do. She descended the basement stairs, opened the heavy iron fire door on the coal furnace and tossed in the buttons, the jacket, and the remnants of the band. The knob of her nose was red, and her eyes were wet when she returned to the kitchen. "Go play now, honey," she urged.

I wonder if any other daughter remembers the first time she made her mother cry.

Mine was of then and of there.

# # #

## 40

DIVIDED WE (STILL) STAND

*G*ays are scary people. Not the gay fellow down the street who provides for his parents and carpools his nieces to day care. Or the fellow who landscapes my yard. Or one of the baggers at the grocery store.

It's only the media-hyped homosexual that sometimes makes me cringe and withdraw. Those clusters of erotic exhibitionists captured on camera for our viewing displeasure.

Scurrilous straights cause me discomfort. But vulgar gays make me feel ashamed.

Harvey Fierstein has expressed impatience with people like me. He once called us "leeches" sitting silently on the sidelines while proud gays pave the way to equal rights for the majority of us "slackers."

I like Harvey a lot. I admire and respect him for his courage and integrity. I think he's a superb actor and writer and a fine role model. He gives gays spirit.

But I don't think he understands that most of us don't want

to be enslaved by the duplicities of straight society. We don't want to clone our ethics, or edit our emotions, or conform our lives to any corrupted concept of happily ever after.

If I could sit down with Harvey Fierstein, I'd tell him I've been hopelessly in love with the same woman for 49 years. But we won't wed, not even though we've worked to support those who choose to, nor because the Supreme Court made marriage equality a reality.

Because, for most of my generation, love is our legacy. Not marriage. We aren't joined by dowry, arrangement, prestige, or necessity. We aren't bound by license, law, or nuptial contract. We don't stay together for the sake of religion, parents, children, social stigma, economics, or expediency.

We're connected only by love. Since time began, love has been the invariable code of our culture. And since love is holy, what we have is sacred.

So, I'd assure Harvey that — even though the alleged "gay agenda" sought to stir all of us into the debauchery of a marriage melting pot — wedlock wasn't the priority of our majority. It wasn't even our American dream. Our culture was once more valuable, valiant, imaginative, romantic, and hopeful than that.

I'd tell Harvey we dreamt of the day when gay men, who have the highest rate of disposable income in America, stopped wasting their resources on purchasing the promise of eternal youth and utilized it to create safe havens in the heartland instead. We imagined gay doctors, nurses, therapists, and health care officials joining forces to build medical centers. Gay lawyers combining talents to establish legal firms. Gay singers and comedians backing gay-owned-and-operated restaurants and nightclubs. Gay athletes creating gay health complexes. Gay financiers building banks. Gay actors starting theaters. Gay educators forming charter schools. Gay religious leaders developing denominations that embrace gay people by interpreting ancient text in the spirit of divine law.

Our desire was to cultivate our culture, not to abolish it. To elevate, not to assimilate. To create, not to copy. To lead, not to follow. To record our history, not to erase it.

I'd question Harvey as to the purpose of new laws, when the constitutional law of equality has not yet been fully upheld for all Americans, guaranteeing life, liberty, and the pursuit of happiness as inalienable.

I'd wonder aloud why we continue to chase after a society that doesn't rise to the talent and tenderness of our own. Why we insist on being accepted by those who haven't earned our respect. Why the blessing of love isn't regarded as its own reward. And why we must diminish the sanctity of ourselves by kowtowing to those who quietly curse us.

Finally, I'd extend my arms in friendship to Harvey Fierstein, asking his pardon on behalf of all us (perceived) leeches marching proudly, quietly, differently, but wholeheartedly beside him. Because I think he understands we hold these truths to be self-evident: That cowards follow the crowd. That courage follows the heart. That virtue makes equality inevitable.

And that straights are scary people — *too.*

# # #

## 41

CHRISTMASTIDE

$\mathcal{C}$LEONE'S FAVORITE SONG was *Joy to the World* directed by the Philharmonic Orchestra and sung by the Mormon Tabernacle Choir. She'd begin playing it as a daybreak reveille on December 12th and continued through the morning of her birthday, December 27th.

We were reminded of the fifteen-day musical salute while driving Elizabeth's mother back to Arkansas in November 1990.

"How come I don't remember this tradition, Mom?"

"You're never home for the holidays more than a day or two, Elizabeth Ann. Besides, your daddy and I only began it after you left home."

During those long gone thirty years since Elizabeth's father died, Cleone remarried several times. As a southern lady rooted in Montgomery, Alabama, she was raised to believe a woman's life wasn't complete without a man in hand. Her current husband of ten years, Bill had been confined to a nursing home, diagnosed with violent hysterical dementia. He hadn't recognized her (or anyone) for six months and never would again, but that didn't stop Cleone from visiting him daily, ignoring his foul-mouthed curses and dodging food spat in her direction.

We promised to stay with her through Thanksgiving, but our plans changed after she asked me to sort through stacks of Bill's personal papers to determine if any needed keeping.

The first item of interest I came across was his association with a local white supremacist group. He kept Nazi propaganda, recruitment paraphernalia, racist hate tapes and a loaded .38 in his desk drawer next to a box of hollow point bullets. I immediately incinerated everything burnable and buried the gun in his asparagus garden. Other discoveries were as serious.

"Mom," I tiptoed, "it says here Bill used your Certificates of Deposit and savings as collateral for the mortgage to purchase this house."

"He promised they'd be safe until the house is paid off."

"You're 83, and he's older. The mortgage is for 30 years."

"I guess."

"Who pays the mortgage?"

"It's automatically deducted from my social security check each month."

"You have your own direct deposit checking account?"

"Yes. Mine pays the car loan, utilities, and property taxes, too."

"Why isn't it all deducted from his account?"

"He pays the insurance, charge cards, grocery account, and incidentals." I hesitated just long enough for her to ask, "Why?"

"Well, what's important is I can tell you how to fix what I've found, so there's nothing for you to get upset about. Since you have his health proxy and financial power of attorney — over his very sizable bank accounts, I must say — it's merely a matter of shuffling funds."

"Meaning?"

"You have the authority to write checks."

By then, both Cleone and Elizabeth were eager for details and had pulled chairs up to the table where I was working.

"Mom, your name isn't on the mortgage, deed to the house, or car title. If Bill should suddenly die, the house and car go directly to his son. His Will leaves his savings and all his belongings to his son. The executor to his estate is his son. His life insurance policy names only his son."

"What about me?" Cleone asked, matter-of-factly.

"He made no provisions for you, Mom."

"Do you think his son knows any of this?"

"According to these letters, he does."

I let that sink in between mother and daughter while I ran some figures and finalized a plan.

After breakfast, the three of us dressed for success in matching hot pink sweatsuits and strings of vintage pearls before descending on the bank where Cleone paid off the mortgage and car loan from Bill's savings account. Once her CDs were released and there was no longer a lien on her savings, she transferred all automatic deductions for household expenses from her checking account to his. Finally, she removed his name as survivor from her accounts and left the bank, unencumbered.

"How do you feel, Mom?" Elizabeth asked.

"Free," she answered.

We stayed on until the 9th of December, gadding about town, buying and wrapping Christmas presents, lighting her ceramic tree, delivering cookies, addressing cards, and confirming plans for Cleone to move to Florida to take up residence in our home after the first of the year.

"Are you sure you don't want to drive back with us now," Elizabeth hoped.

"No, dear. I want to spend the holidays here with my Bridge club and church group. It gives me time to say a more leisurely goodbye."

"Are you okay?"

"Better than okay, Elizabeth. I'm having fun!"

It took us three days to drive home. We arrived on Cleone's birthday, greeted by a cheerful message on our answering machine from her. I immediately dialed her back, putting the phone on speaker.

Cleone's next door neighbor answered.

"Your mom called for an ambulance. The driver swore he got here within a minute. He knew her from church and around town. Everyone loved your mom."

Knew.

Loved.

We sped back to Arkansas.

After arranging her funeral and hosting a large reception, we had Cleone's casket returned to Montgomery where we provided her with a second funeral attended by 135 of her friends and remaining relatives. Internment was next to Elizabeth's father in a small, historic burial ground where all their ancestors also rested. A second reception followed.

The next morning, Elizabeth and I returned to the cemetery a final time.

It was a serene, unseasonably warm December day with no breeze blowing nor snow on the ground. We marveled at the height and width of tiers of fresh flowers left on Cleone's grave, in stark contrast to the other mostly ancient tombstones void of any signs of recent visitors, decorated with weather-worn plastic plants, faded flags, or no mark of remembrance at all.

Instinctively, we began removing fresh flowers from her mother's final resting place to spend the next few hours adorning the surrounding graves, one-by-one, until as many sites as possible in the cemetery had a small bouquet.

Then we rolled down all the windows in the car, popped in a cassette, pumped up the volume to maximum, and slowly drove up and down each pathway playing and replaying *Joy to the World*.

\# \# \#

## 42

A FORCE TO BE RECKONED WITH

I WAS ONCE sued by the Town of Huntington, New York, for 7 seven million dollars, plus interest since 1797, with a request of a sentence be imposed on me of one year in jail for my refusal to surrender documents to the town historian, Rufus B. Langhams, who alleged under oath that the documents had been stolen from the Town by colonial employees and kept hidden by their ancestors for 195 years until I was consigned to auction them off along with the contents of the family estate.

Prior to the lawsuit being heard before New York State Supreme Court Justice William L. Underwood, Jr., I was vilified by the print media, shunned by several former friends, slandered by candidates for political office and their operatives, chastised by churchgoers, and kept under surveillance for nearly a year — only to be threatened by an assistant town attorney hiding (after midnight) in the bushes of my front yard, incessantly meowing until I ventured out, concerned. He emerged from the bushes to back me up to my front door while pretending to have a weapon in his pocket that turned out to be rolled up court papers.

I'd been served.

I share this to demonstrate my profound respect for Christine Blasey Ford's testimony before Congress, September 27, 2018, pertaining to Brett Kavanaugh's nomination to the Supreme Court of the United States.

She was nothing shy of courageous.

Few Americans can imagine the resolve it takes to risk one's life and livelihood in order to ensure justice be delivered on behalf of the majority that will not seek it for themselves, nor for the benefit of others, nor for the good of a nation because the fear of retribution makes stepping up perilous.

I suspect Ford did not want to testify. But as an educated citizen with a conscience compelling her to intervene, she understood her freedom of speech would be denied the moment she chose to silence herself and — like all rights guaranteed by our constitution — free speech is guaranteed as each individual's responsibility to protect.

It is *not* an entitlement.

The fact that her testimony involved exposing intimacies secreted by shame as engineered by patriarchal societies to silence women for centuries made her testimony all the more ominous and her decision to testify that much more valiant.

Our demand for her to be heard should have been deafening. Our cry should have been, "Can you hear us now?"

. . .

As I recall, three attorneys were provided to plead the town's case before Judge Underwood, in chambers, asking him to admonish me for costing the taxpayers (what was alleged to be) a million dollars to argue the merits of their action of replevin in what had become a year long war against me. They called for my incarceration, demanded I turn over all the original town documents in my possession, urged that I be fined, and asked that I be assigned all legal fees and court costs.

I sat alone, acting on my own behalf, as evidence of my innocence.

I presented a book on special loan to me from the reference section of the Huntington Public Library, authored by the town historian Rufus Langhams. Published a decade earlier, it contained photographs of every document I harbored that he'd sworn had been stolen during colonial times, with captions confirming the originals were in his possession and kept locked in the archives of the Huntington Historical Society to which he had sole access.

I submitted letters from several sources attesting to many of those same original documents being sold to them by Rufus Langhams while acting in the capacity of town historian as directed by the Town of Huntington.

I offered to provide a list of names, addresses, and phone numbers of other town residents who were coerced into surrendering copies of inherited documents to Rufus Langhams when he showed up at their homes and demanded them, citing the New York State Property Tort of Replevin as his legal right to confiscate heirlooms.

I contended the documents in my possession were copies

from 195 years passed, not the originals of documents that Langhams sold to profit himself over his many years of incumbency as the Town of Huntington historian.

Supreme Court Justice William L. Underwood, Jr. immediately dismissed the charges against me with prejudice, thereby barring the town from ever bringing an action against me on the claim again and granted me sole property rights before assigning all expenses incurred, court costs, and attorney fees to the Town of Huntington.

I was excused.

The town historian and three town attorneys were all ordered to stay.

To my knowledge, the media never published a retraction, nor was a follow-up story assigned. No acknowledgment of wrongdoing was given by the town attorneys or historian.

The spurious charges in the action lodged against me were never revealed. There was no further discussion of the papers in question.

I was never offered an apology.

Eventually, a friend within Town government told me that, in lieu of no one else wanting the job, Rufus Langhams would remain as town historian but ceased to be trusted with unaccompanied access to historic documents and a full accounting of the archives had been ordered.

Eight years later, the town historian died of a heart attack. His obituary read in part: "Rufus Buford Langhams of Huntington, L.I., once went to England seeking to collect $15,000 in Revolutionary War debts from the British Chancellor of the Exchequer. He was not successful."

I was once a force to be reckoned with.
　　Christine Blasey Ford is one.
　　Shouldn't we all be?

# # #

## 43

HAPPY TRAILS TO YOU

"You're always a happy camper," my kid sister, Kate, frequently said to me. "Even from back when. I've seldom seen you when you weren't. Whereas, the rest of us…" She sighs as her claim tapers off — the 'rest of us' being our four older siblings.

It's March of 2015, and we're in her Florida home an hour southeast of mine enjoying faded photographs of her and me during childhood. It's a monochrome-to-Kodachrome procession of us aging over the years corralled in silver and brass frames crowding the desktop in her den.

"You're smiling in more of them than me," I insist.

"But even when you *aren't*, you're happy!"

She's right. In every print she's kept of me, I stand guilty as charged, picture-proof that regardless of the rocks life hurled at me, I caught them as stones and skimmed them as pebbles across blue waters. Setbacks, solutions, and silver linings have always ruled my world in that way.

Kate triumphs, too, but does it differently. Unlike me (be it a word, a look, or an action) she wounds easily and holds onto the hurt as lifeblood. She can recite the time, place, and reason for every hurt she was forced to endure and slight she perceived from others, intentional or not. She suffers the "slings and arrows" of both fortune and misfortune.

Her self-esteem rarely rides on an even keel, which is reflected in her self-deprecating sense of humor where she always casts herself as the ugly duckling and also-ran. As children, she shadowed me like a stray puppy seeking approval. When we became teenagers and she'd sprouted to be the much-taller *of* the two of us, Kate began rolling her shoulders forward and slumping to avoid attention. But not with only me. She took a back seat in all her outings with friends. She never challenged authority. She eagerly catered to the whims and wishes of others. She refused to go to her junior prom with a boy she had a crush on unless I agreed to find a date and go with her. (I did.) She always worked harder to strive higher because she felt, in doing so, maybe, just maybe, someone would love her.

I don't think she's ever accepted that everyone *does* love her — not because she played a great game of league softball for nine years, or bested those at any table where board games ruled, or succeeded at every task she undertook, or graduated from college summa cum laude, or even when she became an enviable executive at Sony-Columbia Pictures in Hollywood enjoying the daily company of celebrities — but because she is without guile. She's soft-spoken and generous. She's never late to arrive for anything. She's decisive and dependable. She is the first to answer the call, to offer her time, and to provide for others whether asked of, or needed, or not. Her meek demeanor matches her downy curls and wise gray eyes the shade of a Russian Blue.

She's also a coincidental copycat. Although Kate once lived 3,000 miles away for a decade, she would somehow manage to buy the same label slacks, sweaters, and shoes that I wore, paint her rooms the same colors as mine, be partial to the same movies and songs, plant the same flowers, and even managed to select the identical holiday cards for my mom, with both hers and mine arriving in the same mail, on the same days for seven years running.

When she moved to Florida eleven years ago, she arrived in the make and model of car I drove. Eventually, she gave me that car and added my name to the title of her next one so I could have it someday without any fuss. It's what I'll be driving soon.

It's what I'm driving at.

Kate visits us regularly, making the trip to spend the day with her gal pal, my Elizabeth. They leave within hugs after she arrives to scan pawn shops and scour garage sales, saying when they'll be back bearing gifts, and ordering what they want to eat upon return. I'm left behind to be chief cook, baker, bottle washer and decider of the games we'll play into the night.

Sometimes, she stays over, but more often twelve hours of each other's company is one-hour shy of perfection. Before she leaves, we belt out a chorus of, "Happy trails to you, until we meet again" as we did while in our matching cowgirl outfits, sitting on the floor in front of the Sylvania set during the 1950s, joining Roy Rogers and Dale Evans in their signature song. Then I wait by the phone until she gets home and calls to say she's safe and sound.

My dear, beloved, sweet little sister, Baby Kate.

So imagine my surprise when, after a splendid celebration for her 67th birthday on January 22nd, followed by wishes exchanged three weeks later on Valentine's Day (where plans were finalized for my Elizabeth's birthday on February 24th), she called to say, "I'll be there. I'm looking forward to it. But…"

Kate had felt nauseous with a sharp pain in her side. Assuming it was her gallbladder, she visited a clinic around the corner that ordered blood tests and a subsequent ultrasound revealing liver cancer. The following week, an MRI found pancreatic and bile duct cancer. A PET scan upped the ante to bone and spinal column cancer after more tests confirmed the cancer was *everywhere*.

No, this is not the kind of diagnosis that responds to operations, chemotherapy, radiation, clinical trials, experimental drugs, or immunotherapy. Hers is the type that robs you of 25 pounds in 25 days and makes you hope for enough time to get your affairs in order.

Nothing seems real now. We act on automatic, listening to orders we don't want to hear and filling out forms we're forced into finishing as if any of it matters more than these last precious weeks, days, hours, minutes, seconds spent together.

When she asks me to translate the results of her latest tests, I relay a bowdlerized truth, and she listens with an editor's ear, both of us trying to alter the inevitable.

If it were me, there would be livid levity. Instead, it's Kate, who embraces the prospect of dying and counts on me to be there for a final cowgirl singalong.

"Yes," I smiled when she asked it of me. "As if wild horses could drag me away."

But I am not a happy camper.

# # #

Kathleen May Cantine (Baby Kate) died on May 16, 2015, seventy-seven days after first being diagnosed with pancreatic cancer. She was 67.

4 4

SIGH CRIMES & MISDEMEANORS

*T*he first flawed decision I made to indicate the direction I was heading resulted from letting my kid sister, Kate, annoy me. I was 3.7 at the time and half-pint-size for my age; she was a dissident at 2.4 and well on her way to being bigger and brighter than me.

We lived in a house on the brick street of a southside neighborhood in a small midwestern town where her crib sat in my parent's bedroom being used one night to corral us while company visited. It was late. We were lying back-to-back. I was weary and wanting to sleep.

"Get out! Get out! Get out! Get out!" she incessantly demanded. It was *her* bed, and I wasn't welcomed even though I wasn't sleeping there voluntarily. Finally, I got fed up and gave her a reason to bellyache. I wet the bed.

That was my crime.

As punishment, every person Kate introduced me to from that night forward included the lead-in, "This is my sister,

Margie. When we were kids, she peed on me," invariably prompting the retelling of our toddler turf war.

The last time she introduced me was to her late shift hospice nurse in May of 2015. It allowed her to maintain the upper hand on my heart forevermore.

When I was six the teacher asked me to read in front of the class while she stepped out to confer with a parent. After she left, Clem Molar ran up and kissed me. When the teacher returned, my classmates all squealed what had happened.

That was my crime.

As punishment, the teacher blamed me for Clem's insolence and banished me me to the cloakroom for the rest of the day.

I never forgave him.

In junior high school, my best friend was Beverly Brown. During the summer of 1959, we'd frequent the Bloomfield Elementary School playground where most the neighborhood kids hung out. One day I discovered the basement door to the school was left open. Upon further exploration, I found I could easily walk through the door of the humongous furnace and crawl through the boiler tunnels leading to classrooms located on the first and second floors.

Inspired, I became an entrepreneur as The Bloomfield Boiler Guide. The plan was to charge a quarter per tour commencing with a Coke & Chips Party in the furnace chamber while whistling to Mitch Miller's *The River Kwai* blaring repetitively on Bev's Stromburg Carlson portable record player.

That was my crime.

At the end of the trial run tour, we were greeted by police officers as we, one-by-one, gaily emerged from the furnace before being transported by patrol cars to 'the joint' with sirens screaming all the way. Once there, we were sentenced to sitting on hard benches until our parents arrived to spring us.

Bev's parents came within minutes. Mine never did. After several hours, a change in shift occurred, and I was released to walk home as my claim to chain gang fame crumbled.

At age 14, I forged my parent's signatures to wangle a coveted 37-hour-a-week job working 5-hour weeknights and 12-hour Saturdays as the record department sales and inventory control clerk at Hopkins, the most popular electronics store in town.

The Hopkins family consisted of the Magooish father, Robert, Sr., who was obsessed with soybeans, and two feuding brothers, Motorola Bob and Prince John, the latter being a local disc jockey who depended on me to choose the best of the latest released demo records arriving daily in the mail for playing on his prime time radio show. All three men were members of the Kiwanis Club that placed a freestanding, glass globe, stainless steel Ford Gumball machine at the entrance to my music department.

Ford gumballs came in pristine white, cadmium yellow, royal blue, Pepto pink, and verdant green, each with a fiend thirsty flavor cementing a brisk business as the best penny chews of the '50s and '60s.

Records were a buck plus one cent tax to the dollar for 45s, so Magoo kept plenty of pennies on the top of the cash register to pay the tax for any customer short of change.

As it so happened, I was addicted to Ford gumballs. I used the freebie pennies (and a few from the till) to treat my multi-record-buying customers to a gumball without thinking to inform the trio.

That was my crime.

Many miles and decades later, I learned the missing Lincolns — sometimes as many as twenty a day — were wreaking havoc each evening when Motorola Bob cashed out the register and came up short against the receipts. He swore Prince John was stealing change to keep the books from ever balancing. The discourse turned so beastly between accusations and denials that one day Prince John packed up his family and moved to Texas.

My punishment was in learning I was the trigger, much too late to rectify the situation. Not that Motorola Bob would have admitted any error and not that Prince John would have accepted any apology and not that Magooish cared beyond the ticker tape apparatus next to the gumball machine operating 24/7/365 tracking the soybean market.

As a corporate executive in New York City for the designer line of the largest provider of leisurewear in the nation, I'd occasionally gift a sample pair of pajamas 'borrowed' from the showroom for delivery to a very wealthy friend who pestered me for a freebie each time she planned a new paramour sleepover.

That was my crime.

One day, I was served with a subpoena to appear in court to testify as "the other women" in a high profile NYC divorce proceeding. It seemed the wife of my friend's lover had discovered her husband's affair and promised not to divorce him if he told her the name of his mistress.

Unbeknownst to me, my friend suggested her lover give the wife *my* name instead of hers, thereby allowing them to continue the affair without consequence. Hubby complied, never suspecting his wife would use the confession as proof of his infidelity, backfiring on all three of them once I was deposed.

That was my cure.

Because life is a silver lining for those of us willing to scrape the surface of adversity.

By age six, I'd begun to sense how oppression is forged from the indignation of adults. Being unfairly punished was pivotal in teaching me to observe more, listen closely, talk less, read sooner, recognize the treachery of treachery, and understand that misogyny won't be curtailed from the child up until it's eradicated from the adult down.

As for those men in blue wearing badges? It's true that I still challenge authority. But I never again got caught breaking into another school, and I make it my purpose to shake the hand of all police officers I encounter, thanking them for their service while trying to refrain from whistling *The River Kwai* as I work the crowd.

Meanwhile, the mere mention of gumballs requires I battle

temptations to buy a vintage Ford machine on eBay as a tribute to Motorola Bob, Prince John, and Magooish, who taught me the invaluable skills that eventually landed me a job in Manhattan where I sang *New York, New York* with gusto after turning the head of Ol' Blue Eyes when we passed as strangers in the night outside the 21 Club.

Which takes me to the brink of divorce court with one of the most interesting and exciting bad influences I ever had the endless pleasure of knowing — and leaves me within the aura of my sister Kate, who remained my cherished friend and laughter cohort for the rest of her life.

# # #

THIS DIAMOND RING

I DON'T KNOW if it was so for my three brothers, but whenever we three sisters asked Mom what she wanted for Mother's Day, her birthday, or Christmas, she'd invariably say, "A diamond ring, a fur coat, and a trip around the world."

Nowadays, such requests may not seem that unreasonable, what with seven-year-olds pocketing iPhones, college students making pilgrimages, and fur coats being faked well enough to warrant splattering by PETA paint. But back in the '50s, '60s, and '70s, these were all big-ticket items for the vast majority of American women.

Since Mom wasn't elitist, extravagant, or pretentious, I didn't take her wish list seriously. She had a mink-ish stole she dearly loved, but only wore from time to time. She managed to group-trip-travel to every country and place she ever dreamt of going before she passed away just shy of 93. And she appeared satisfied with wearing her wedding ring during 31 years of marriage and 37 years of widowhood — a millimeter thin band of yellow gold originally mounted with seven minuscule diamond chips, two of them missing from forever ago.

"This diamond ring doesn't shine for me anymore," she'd chime along with the Gary Lewis and the Playboys 1965 hit and still being played in 1979, a decade into her widowhood.

"Are you planning on taking it off and selling it?" I once asked.

"No," she admitted. "Remember, dear, the first ring represents your beginning and shouldn't cost more than what you can safely afford. The last ring shows how far you've gotten. It may weigh more, and the stone might be bigger — but that ring is less about who you are and more about who you *think* you are."

Costume jewelry was more Mom's style, mostly matched sets of necklaces and bracelets with complementing clip-on earrings, pin-back cloth flowers, rhinestone studded hair combs, and watches with exchangeable bands. It was while rummaging through these, tangled together in an old cedar box stamped Souvenir of Gaylord, Michigan, that I detected the faint fragrance of her Yardley Lavender still lingering there as I matched each pretty piece of paste to memories of the outfit she wore and the special occasion that warranted the wearing.

That is, except for one out-of-place, unfamiliar, etched gold band with a solitaire diamond setting that seemed a perfect starter ring for a young (or young-at-heart) someone who hoped to commit, or celebrate a first anniversary, or wear on the pinky until presenting it as a simple act of friendship to another.

It's a dainty little ring, perfectly capable of stirring up tender emotions — but one I'd never wear, since it wasn't given to me by my lifelong love, nor claimed as known by any family member.

It prompted me to let someone else create a warm memory by my giving the ring away. No strings attached. No expectations of return. Quietly and without adieu, certain that Mom would approve.

Because it wasn't as if I gave her wedding ring away. Never!

That tarnished band of gold has resided on my pinky since she passed in 2006 and will remain there until I do as a testament to the woman whose namesake I am, and the cherished memories of her I wouldn't sacrifice — not even for a diamond ring, a fur coat, and a trip around the world.

# # #

46

INTERVIEW ON BEING A MISFIT

Q: Have you had much professional rejection?

A: I seldom submit what I write; however, when I have, then yes, I've received rejections.

Q: Any favorites?

A: A friend once told me that humor written by women is almost always tossed when sent to *The New Yorker* for their *Shouts and Murmurs* feature.

Q: You don't aim low, do you?

A: Big dreamers rarely do. Anyhow, after hearing that, I got on my high-horse one Saturday night and submitted a *Shouts* piece, thinking it would be at the top of the editor's mailbox for consideration on Monday morning.

Q: And?

A: I got an instant — and when I say instant, I mean within seconds — an *instant* rejection followed by an email from the desk of Bob Mankoff offering me a subscription to *The New Yorker* at a discounted price.

Q: Ouch?

A: Actually, I burst out laughing and immediately thought about contacting The Guinness Book of Records to see if it set a world rejection record.

Q: Have you?

A: No. But the thought still percolates. More important is, it put the magazine into perspective for me. It finally makes sense as to why *The New Yorker* is thinning.

Q: Because?

A: Because writers are readers first and foremost, so when you alienate a writer — even a bad writer — you risk losing a reader.

Q: You stopped reading *The New Yorker*?

A: Except when someone gives me a copy, yes. But to be fair, it was drudgery for me to understand most the articles. Many a night, suffering from insomnia, a story in *The New Yorker* has put me right to sleep.

Q: How about your novel, *Imogene's Eloise*? Was that accepted right off?

A: Exactly the opposite.

Q: Seriously?

A: Yes. And let me stress — *thankfully*.

Q: Can you elaborate?

A: I trusted it to one of the owners of an LGBT publishing house whom I regarded as a friend. I wasn't really looking for a contract so much as a nod.

Q: Approval.

A: More like guidance. I hoped to be told it appeared promising. At 150,000 words, I already knew it was too long. I was looking to be told to resubmit it when I edited it by half. Something more of that nature.

Q: And you got what?

A: After following the submission guidelines, I got a sloppily composed email thanking me for my short story and saying they had no interest in it.

Q: A 150,000-word short story? You're kidding.

A: Exactly. And I am not. But like the email from Bob Mankoff, I've benefited from the rejection.

Q: Are you and the publisher still friends?

A: No, but not because of that.

Q: Because of…?

A: It's not relevant.

Q: But it is an interviewers prerogative, so…

A: Yes. Yes it is. And I do so love the word, prerogative. Okay. A third party had told me, she decided not to submit to my former friend's publishing house because she wanted to be represented by a suit.

Q: A suit?

A: Someone who always looked spit-shined, ironed, successful, and worthy of her writing rather than disheveled, wrinkled, and as crumpled as this publishing person sometimes appeared in public. So when the topic of submissions arose between us, I said I was privy to something that I thought would be beneficial for her to know, but made her promise not to tell, or ever identify me, should she choose to bring the issue up for discussion. When she agreed, I related the impression her partner's sloppiness made and added that I thought it valid for a writer to expect her publisher to always look professional.

Q: And she told?

A: Yes, but it wasn't that she told. It was that, after she betrayed my confidence, she lied to me about betraying me, repeatedly, until she finally admitted she lied, but in doing so, justified the betrayal and the lying, then compounded the lie by being deceitful about another author whom she predicted might cross her. I cut ties with her for that, and it cost me the loss of up to nine of her publisher colleagues.

Q: Surely, that bothered you.

A: Not really. I'm far better off because of it, and I believe it's what people who allow themselves to be bullied don't understand. Whatever you think you might lose in the short run, you gain in the long term, and the people you end up with are so much more valuable than those who turned away.

Q: Food for thought or preachy?

A: I'm certainly no stranger to bandwagons, but I'd prefer to think of myself as someone who sets an example by my actions speaking louder than my words.

Q: That's a perfect Segway back to role models. What do you think of the way women are portrayed?

A: In?

Q: LesFic books and movies.

A: If you mean lump sum, all genres, that's really too sweeping a question. Even then, I'd be limited to the books I've read and the movies I've seen.

Q: Most movies are based on books, so let's start with the movies.

A: I have trouble finding myself in them, of my experiences as a woman, as a friend, as a lover, as an employee, as a person.

Q: As opposed to, what? Finding yourself in straight movies?

A: Heavens no. I mean, I could see some of myself in the lead character of, say, *Norma Rae*, from when I was younger and involved in fighting for change, and in *Kissing Jessica Stein*, to the extent of her wanting something different than what she was being offered. Except for the opening, I enjoyed that film immensely by the way.

Q: The opening?

A: A leading female character having backroom sex with a man before she seduces a woman. It's like the required stamp of approval for all lesbian-themed films — that the film is only worthy of attention, or more worthy because a man staked his claim *first* and foremost.

Q: How about *The L Word*?

A: I watched it for the first year but, again, I couldn't relate. Like most Americans who feel there's no one in Congress speaking for them, I think the vast majority of homosexual women feel the same about movies. What's on the screen bears little resemblance to their everyday lives and much deeper emotions. It might be a gender gap trap to even say so, but I often think boomers represent the last great generation of romantic music and gestures before nameless hookups and STDs became the norm.

Q: Do you miss that time?

A: I can't miss what I've continued to maintain for myself. But I miss it for younger women who've never had an opportunity to experience it or make an informed choice in favor of it over the fragility and transience of modern relationships.

Q: Do you think younger women would be interested in the world of your youth?

A: I'd like to think they'd embrace the good of it — like they embrace the remake of great songs by younger artists — and choose to establish a romantic lifestyle for themselves.

Q: Your book, *Imogene's Eloise*, is primarily a reminder of where our culture was, isn't it?

A: No, it's not just about where we've been. It's about how we got to where we are in a patriarchal, primarily Christian identified, mostly divided society where women are in the majority. It's about discovering where our minds and hearts were then, in contrast with how the minds and hearts of today interpret back then. It's about how our 'in-the-life' world within the overall world has changed dramatically.

Q: Through the journey of a single love affair?

A: Actually, there are many love affairs going on of varying intensities between numerous people in the book. It's about recognizing the differences between love and lust and under-standing the degrees of friendship.

Q: Sex?

A: Romantic to incite the imagination without being explicit. It also teaches history without the drudgery and is entertaining without it having been written strictly for enter-tainment value.

Q: What do you think is most appealing about *Imogene's Eloise*?

A: Readers decide that on an individual basis. But the intent is to expose the commonalities we share pertaining to those we love and how it's what everyone, at some juncture in their lives, wishes for — what most are told they cannot have.

I'm telling the reader you *can* have it. That, on some level, to some extent, you are in this book, and someone you know, someone you want to know, and someone you long to meet is in this book. There are emotions you've felt, thoughts you've had, and answers you seek to questions in the back of your mind. And just like life, you'll applaud some, resist others, and ponder the rest.

Q: Any reactions?

A: It's a marathon read at 383 pages, so the 53 reviews have trickled in as people cross the finish line. But so far, primarily applause. One who didn't like it admitted she didn't read it before leaving a review. Another left a review who, obviously, hadn't read it, but didn't admit it. Such people are unavoidable.

Q: How about your beta readers?

A: I didn't employ beta readers. I'm not certain I believe in writing as a team sport. But I did offer a peek to blog followers before I edited the book down for a final time.

Q: And?

A: Very supportive. Except, once I had a person, I wish I could remember her name, she sampled the first ten chapters of my book and said — and I'm paraphrasing here — "The characters are weak. I only read books about strong women." So I thanked her for her opinion and moved on. But I wish now I'd reminded her that women aren't born strong. It's not a given for us. And back in the day, we didn't have parents, siblings, magazines, movies, advertisements to encourage us, or fictionalized characters toting guns and giving men karate chops as our pacifiers. We grew strong in spite of naysayers and obstacles. And the women coming of age in the '50s and '60s — those women who grew up being denied loans and credit cards, denied the right to buy a house without a male co-sign, denied the right to sell inherited property without a man's permission, denied jobs advertised as help wanted male, denied justice in our courts, denied protection from violence, denied entrance to colleges and clubs, denied the right to run for political office, denied the right to be heard, denied advancement in the workplace, denied equal pay, denied consideration or equality under the law by both government and religion — those women of that second-class American society who fought to guarantee our first-class American citizenship — *they're* the strong ones. *Those* are the characters that should serve as your role models. And until that's understood — honey — you haven't a clue as to what the meaning of the word 'strong' truly is.

Q: You're published in paperback and on Kindle. Why?

A: Two reasons. First, 85% of all books sold are on Kindle or other electronic devices. And Amazon offers a free app that turns every computer, tablet, and phone into an electronic reader. That's a big incentive.

Q: The genre is romance.

A: Because Amazon and Bowkers require it.

Q: Given more of a choice?

A: It's a dramedyherstoryromance.

Q: *Imogene's Eloise* is subtitled as inspired by a true-love story. Tell me, how much of it is true?

A: More of it than not. Certainly all the best parts.

# # #

## 47

AND THE REST IS MYSTERY

I'd nicknamed her AK-57 for the year she was born, a moniker that wasn't lost on Amanda Kyle Williams, who fostered a droll, flippant sense of humor about herself, the world at large and...oh yeah...serial killers.

We were wired (as I believe everyone is) through happenstance.

In 2012, I was asked by a mutual friend to add my name to a list of those vying for a chance to win a free copy of William's recently released hit novel, *The Stranger You Seek*, even though I'm an irremediable romantic who avoids most media pertaining to violence. In fact, I'd never read a mystery — not even *In Cold Blood* by Truman Capote whose other works are all favorites of mine.

So I was a tad taken aback when Amanda friended me on Facebook to say I'd won a copy of her novel and asked me to provide shipping information to Bantam Books.

I immediately confessed to my disinterest in reading

mysteries but ended up agreeing to making her the one exception to my rule after learning we had more than being wordsmiths in common. Big things like our love for animals, rescuing dogs, and the feeding of feral cats. Little things like the linoleum of her entryway being the identical pattern to that on the kitchen floor of the first apartment I'd ever leased. And other things like how she'd signed with the same literary agency that rejected my query, we both had a Pekingese named Bella, we'd both been private detectives, and we each had a cat that threatened us within an inch of our toes and nose on a daily basis.

She'd requested my brutally honest opinion of her book, so I gave it: No, her account of Atlanta didn't make me want to visit. Yes, her description of the Carolina coast tempted me to move there. I'd warned her that I prided myself in using my delusional chess expertise to predict plots ahead of endings. She humbled me by proving I hadn't a clue as to who the killer in *Stranger* was until being astounded during the final pages.

But our lives were seldom similar otherwise. She had difficulty reading because of dyslexia; I am a voracious reader without afflictions. She lost a parent at a young age following her mother's slow decline. My mom passed instantly as I turned sixty. The love of her life succumbed to a malignancy after their twenty years together. My love affair still flourishes at forty-nine.

Yet we both understood how it felt to lose a cherished sibling after providing steadfast care during their inevitable demise, just as we both knew my combat against heart disease is pure child's play compared to her valiant fight against cancer, truly life's most insidious serial killer.

Amanda Kyle Williams lost her battle on Friday morning, August 31, 2018, two weeks after turning 61. And although we never actually met face-to-face, eye-to-eye, shoulder-to-shoulder, or toe-to-toe, we existed as tongue-in-cheek and heart-to-heart kindred spirits for six remarkable years.

Losing her saddened me deeply.

\# \# \#

48

CELEBRITY RECALLS

I rode in my first limousine on New Year's Eve, 1973. Our friend, Tom Dale, was a market research specialist and producer of television commercials who lived in a penthouse on East 48th Street and needed to be seen on the town with arm candy as a guise for his true closeted self. Elizabeth and I were his go-to-gal-pals and happily so. It afforded us the luxury to eat at the most trendy restaurants, attend posh events, and have third-row orchestra seats on the aisle. That New Year's Eve, we'd seen *Pippin'* at The Music Box Theater on West 45th Street.

The show let out after throngs had already gathered in Times Square anticipating the ball dropping at midnight to welcome the start of 1974. At some point, the limo needed to cross Broadway. When the police separated the crowds enough for traffic from the theater district to pass through, the people began to touch the darkened windows, hoping to get a glimpse of a celebrity hidden inside.

At that moment, I realized how much more we identified with those revelers freezing on the outside of the limo than we'd ever be like the bigwigs they presumed to be riding within. I've never ceased wondering who's hidden behind the tinted windows of limousines — but I stopped assuming it was anyone famous long, long ago.

Three weeks later, after attending Liza Minnelli's *Live At The Winter Garden,* we joined Tom's chum, Ted, for dinner at his private table in Ted Hook's Backstage Restaurant next door to the Martin Beck Theater. Besides being a former hoofer in the chorus of more than 400 movies, Ted served as Talulah Bankhead's personal secretary for five years and regularly entertained friends and customers with intimate stories of the megastar.

Seated next to my Liz and directly across from me was Wayland Flowers of Wayland & Madam fame. Madam was a pink wood puppet head-to-waist that looked like an exaggerated Gloria Swanson's character in the movie *Sunset Boulevard.* Unlike our friend Tom, Wayland Flowers was unabashedly gay and out about it. His act, like his performance at the dinner table with Madam seated to his left, was bewitching. But when dinner was served he stuck Madam head first into a brown paper bag, as if she wasn't *alive* to the rest of us. (Oddly enough, I never quite came to terms with that.)

Wayland Parrott Flowers was a creative genius of natural quick wit. He died October 11, 1988, of AIDS at age 48.

Ted Hook was a sparkling personality who was the personification of instant entertainment. He died July 19, 1995, of AIDS at age 65.

Thomas Bryon Dale died in 2007. He was 76. I don't know

exactly when, or of what. No notice was placed on his behalf, nor acknowledgment made of his passing. It wasn't until his brother's obituary was published many years later that Tom was mentioned as having preceded his brother in death. Tom said they'd always been estranged. In that respect, he remained closeted to the end.

Liza Minnelli's show closed after a 20-day run.

I've never been attracted to men, but I have always been egocentric about their attraction to me.

One afternoon, while returning to my job on Fifth Avenue, a strikingly handsome man passed me by. Certain I knew him, I turned my head to spot him looking back. We smiled, waved, and continued on.

Hours later, while scanning books at Barnes & Noble, we met again, both of us demonstratively delighted to see the other.

"I think we might have gone to school together," I said, shaking his hand while introducing myself.

"That must be it!" he grinned back. "I'm Hugh O'Brian."

Hugh O'Brian (*The Life and Legend of Wyatt Earp*) was born in Rochester, New York, 1925. I was born twenty-one years later in Michigan. It was an honest, mistake given the circumstances. After all, at nine years old and for three years thereafter, his was my favorite black-and-white television western.

I first met Walter Leyden Brown while temporarily bunking at my brother Michael's 49 Prince Street fifty dollar a month, three-room with a water closet, 6th-floor tenement walk-up. Michael was a student at the Royal Academy of Dramatic Arts in London at the time.

After I moved uptown, Walter began the staging of a three-night production of his play, *No Way In*, at the La Mama Theater. The day before opening night, the actress cast as Character Number One got a paying role elsewhere and quit Walter's show. Desperate, he asked me to take over the non-speaking role of the pole-swirling woman. I was a student at the American Academy of Dramatic Arts then, so eagerly accepted.

Although he directed (and we'd rehearsed) a one circle spin with a cry of a lady in distress, on opening night, I swung wide and long, screaming like a banshee.

A critic for *The Village Voice* was in the audience. The next day, his review panned the director, the play and the cast, except for my performance, which he applauded for scaring the bejesus out of him.

Because his only child was starring in the play, Claude Rains (*The Invisible Man, Casablanca, Notorious, Mr. Skeffington*) was also in the audience with his friends, Roscoe Lee Brown (*The Cowboys, Uptown Saturday Night, Jumping' Jack Flash*), and Butterfly McQueen, (*Gone With The Wind, Duel In The Sun*). He motioned me over for introductions and they graciously complimented me on my performance.

The next night, the audience was given notice that Character Number One would be played by an understudy.

Walter Leyden Brown, 49, of 49 Prince Street, New York

City, died August 23, 1988. Before returning to his family home during his final days, he'd confided to friends that he had AIDS.

———

Prior to being cast in *No Way In*, I'd worked as a volunteer at the La Mama Theater for one grease-grill-hot summer day, helping to remove, drag, and reinstall chairs from the old location to the new one. It left me conspicuously grimy, unkempt, and eager to catch subway connections to my upper west side apartment. While crammed shoulder-to-shoulder into a rush hour crowd on a street corner waiting for the WALK sign to free us, I spotted a limousine with a swarm of people catty-corner from me. Turning my head to see if the woman on my right noticed the commotion, I was so stupefied by her beauty that I could barely mumble to the man on my left, "That's Elizabeth Taylor next to me."

He leaned discreetly forward to check.

"Why, yes," said Richard Burton. "Yes, it is."

———

Alice Demovic was the sister of a good friend who (like me) was living foot-loose-and-fancy-free in Manhattan, albeit she resided in a tonier upper east side neighborhood and hobnobbed with a much more affluent crowd. Nevertheless, I was her instant late-late night wing-woman when absolutely no one else was available, and she needed a person to go on the blind side of a double date with her and her current love interest.

One morning just after midnight, I was awakened and told a limo was waiting for me downstairs in front of my apartment on West 85th Street and to chop-chop.

"How shall I dress?" I asked.

"Cute and quickly."

I cannot remember the name of her dinner companion, nor the occasion, but we were all seated stage-side to catch the last set at Rodney ("I don't get no respect.") Dangerfield's. Afterward, Rodney joined us for dinner. He was exactly the same person in real life as the characters he played in *Caddyshack* and *Easy Money*.

Dangerfield was born on the same date as my not-yet-met sweetheart's father, Rufus, and he died on the date of my long-gone father, LaVerne.

During the 1960s and early 1970s, I was street-treated as an attractive young executive working in the 666 Fifth Avenue building bordering New York City's historic 21 Club. Over the years, I'd pivoted heads of Frank Sinatra (heavier set, mid-50s, and balding Ol' Blue Eyes period), George Hamilton (*By Love Possessed, Zorro, The Godfather III,* and easily twenty times better looking in person than portrayed on the silver screen), John Lindsey (NYC Mayor photographed kissing me on Page 2 of the *New York Post* during a campaign re-election rally), and others.

One day, while on my way to lunch with an associate,

Scott, who was obsessed with men's fashion, he said (way too loudly) of the diminutive fellow walking a mere foot in front of us, "That man's suit is so wrinkled it looks like he sleeps in the cargo holds of planes."

Aristotle Onassis' head turned back to glare at us, but he and Scott kept walking as I ground to a halt, glad to lose them both in the passing of pedestrians.

Later that same week, I was within inches of Onassis again.

I'd been visiting Terry, the wife of Michael, at their exquisite Madison Avenue store, M. Comer of London Antiques, when Onassis entered and zeroed in on the small table I was standing next to.

"How much is this?" he inquired of Michael.

"Three thousand dollars."

"Not expensive enough," he waved off.

I've often wondered if Michael had answered "thirty thousand dollars," would Onassis have bought the table, regardless of the actual value?

Years later, while being an animal lover en route to becoming an animal activist, I was walking behind a woman wearing what appeared to be leather pants. I was focused so intently on determining the fabric that I hadn't noticed she'd stopped, causing me to bump into her and knock her off her feet.

"Oh! Excuse me. I'm so sorry, Mrs. Kennedy!" I rattled, mortified, as private security agents rushed to her rescue.

She was married to Onassis at the time.

# # #

ALMOST PARADISE

*D*uring the 29 years we've lived in Florida, we've made few in-the-life friends. It's not that they don't exist in small towns here. (We do.) And it's not that we're ashamed. (We aren't.)

It's that, excluding most metro areas, if you (a) want to feel assured that the police will respond to your call for help in a timely manner and, (b) you want to receive the finest health-care when you're injured or sick and, (c) you want to keep your pets out of harms way and, (d) you want to keep your car from being vandalized and, (e) you want to live in an area where the neighborhood watch looks out for your home and, (f) you want the person working on your teeth to be gentle and, (h) you want to be able to make a living and, (i) you want to avoid having your license plate recorded when attending certain events — then you don't risk outing others whom you think are kindred spirits by drawing attention to their personal lives, even in an effort to make friends.

It's one reason The Pulse nightspot in Orlando was a Mecca for residents and visitors alike. It provided a gay safe haven for fulfilling the need to feel an instant camaraderie accompanying the demonstrative joy of others.

To be honest, we've never actually been to a gay nightclub. While there was a smattering of New York City lesbian bars during the '60s when we were younger, the mixed genders of nowadays clubs with multiple rooms, live bands, separate stages, decks, and professional disc jockeys didn't exist for women.

What we *did* have (aside from a Sebring jukebox at one-gender venues) were summertime tea dances at Cherry Grove and The Pines on Fire Island, mostly male, but with a sufficient showing of Coppertone females to complement the communal glee being shared as disco music blared, connecting us in happiness to every other outdoor dance floor.

Nearly fifty years later, not only are gathering places just as sparse, but on June 12, 2016, a man (whose name doesn't deserve to be remembered by anyone, ever) mass-murdered 49 partygoers at The Pulse Nightclub and wounded 53 others.

It's imperative we note, in March of that same year, then Governor Rick Scott's HB 401 bill died in committee. Had HB 401 passed, it would have allowed doctors, nurses, healthcare providers, and hospitals to refuse treatment to lesbians and gays without fear of facing liability in Florida courts. Based on religious freedom to discriminate, HB 401 was to have taken effect on July 1, 2016.

It's not that healthcare discrimination doesn't occur in places across the nation, but here it would have had the opportunity to exist without the fear of exposure or anyone being held accountable for it.

As a resident of Florida who's been subjected to medical misdiagnosis and nearly killed and billed for it, I always hesitate before seeking help.

Which begs the question: Why do we live in Mother Nature's perfect place among such people?

It's because we believe Orlando's healthcare providers and most Florida facilities are better than disingenuous leaders and sanctimonious legislators.

We believe the inherent good in people will always outweigh the acquired bad.

We believe when vice endeavors to infiltrate, virtue counters with massive resistance.

We believe if deceit sits down on the dais, multitudes will arise to defy demagoguery.

And, too, it's because we know, even if we often weep before we sleep at night, and intermittently weep again for weeks or maybe months or even years to come, love will triumph through however many broken hearts it takes to prevail.

Because it must.

# # #

IMOGENE'S ELOISE: Inspired by a true-love story

by Marguerite Quantaine

383 Pages

The phenomena of love with 67 remarkable characters,

each in the pursuit and touched by the joy of love.

ALWAYS ON AMAZON & IN SELECTED BOOKSTORES

Available in paperback and at the Kindle nearest you.

Marguerite Quantaine is an essayist and author living in Florida. She is currently working on ELOISE'S IMOGENE, book two of a planned IMOGENE'S ELOISE trilogy.

Find her on Amazon
Friend her on Facebook
Follow her on Twitter

---

www.margueritequantaine.com

**My heartfelt thanks to you for reading
Seriously, Mom, you didn't know?**

I'd welcome your questions and comments on Amazon, Facebook, Twitter, or left my website.

Truly,
Marguerite

Made in the USA
San Bernardino, CA
29 May 2020